Susanne Pagoldh

NORDIC KNITTING

THIRTY-ONE PATTERNS IN THE SCANDINAVIAN TRADITION

INTERWEAVE PRESS • LOVELAND   A & C BLACK • LONDON

Translated from the Swedish by Carol Huebscher Rhoades
Technical editing by Theresa Gaffey

First edition Copyright 1987
Susanne Pagoldh/ANFANG PUBLISHERS, INC, STOCKHOLM
Almqvist & Wiksell Printers, Uppsala 1987

English Language Edition Copyright 1991 by
Interweave Press
201 E. Fourth Street
Loveland, Colorado 80537
ISBN 0-934026-68-8

Pagoldh, Susanne, 1956–
     [Stickat från Norden. English]
     Nordic knitting / Susanne Pagoldh.
         p.   cm.
     Includes index.
     ISBN 0-934026-68-8 : $21.95
     1. Knitting--Scandinavia--Patterns.   I. Title
     TT819.S26P3413   1991
     746,9'2--dc20   91-28263
                                                            CIP

Published in Great Britain 1992 by
A & C Black (Publishers) Limited
35 Bedford Row, London WC1R 4JH
ISBN 0 7136 3525 8

A CIP catalogue record for this book is available from the British Library.

CONTENTS

To right: Embroidered gloves from the collection of the National Museum of Iceland (number 1052).
To left: A Selbu sweater from Norway, shown also on page 52. Photo: Susanne Pagoldh. The front cover shows a beaded wrist warmer belonging to Greenland's Women's Union Collection in Nuuk. The title page shows a detail of an embroidered mitten from the National Museum of Iceland (number 5935). The back cover shows a jacket with knitted sleeves. The pattern on the sleeves comes from Enviken in Dalarna, Sweden. The cover's background pattern comes from the Faroe Islands. Photo: Susanne Pagoldh.

TRANSLATOR'S NOTE

My involvement with Scandinavian culture began with a fascination with Ingmar Bergman's films. In a course in Scandinavian culture, the professor said that Swedish was easy to learn, so I taught myself the basic grammar and vocabulary, and eventually progressed enough to enjoy the challenge of reading Sweden's authors in their own language. It was even more fun to read the texts of the Swedish knitting books that Elizabeth Zimmermann supplied. I had already been able to figure out most patterns just from the pictures, but by reading the texts I learned much more about the intricacies of the patterns and the history of Swedish knitted textiles. When I went to Sweden for formal language training, I planned to learn more about traditional textiles at the same time.

Beautifully crafted textiles are part of everyday life in the Nordic countries. There is a timeless quality in the colors and materials which is reflected in the attention to detail taken in the making of the textiles. In weaving, lacemaking, and knitting, working with fine threads and hand finishing seem to be the norm rather than the exception. Traditional patterns abound, sometimes worked in more up-to-date colors. During a winter stay in Uppsala, Sweden, I was quite impressed by the number of people wearing traditionally patterned, handknitted mittens and sweaters. I even spotted a pair or two of mittens made by *nålbinding,* a Scandinavian needleweaving technique.

Knitting proved to be a common and important link between me and the people I met. Many of them thought that an American who knitted was more surprising than one learning Swedish! Perhaps because of knitting's connections between past and present, people and cultures, I've always found reading knitting books to be comforting in the same way that knitting itself is calming. The day I found Susanne Pagoldh's *Nordic Knitting*, I spent the afternoon on a waterfront park bench in central Stockholm just looking at the beautiful pictures and appreciating the nature and traditions that are so much a part of Scandinavian textiles. As the summer went on, the book was my link with Nordic knitting traditions as I sat in my Swedish apartment, knitting the mittens pictured on page 73 with Finnish yarn bought in Helsinki.

The opportunity for translating *Nordic Knitting* came when I took it to show my friend and knitting teacher, Jody Aves, at Interweave's Spin-Off Autumn Retreat. Everyone who saw the book wanted it including, luckily, publisher Linda Ligon. Translating *Nordic Knitting* was a perfect way to combine my scholarly work in Swedish literature and language with my knitting. By working closely with the text, I learned more about Swedish style in both language and craft. All of my Scandinavian translation skills came into play as the book, while primarily written in Swedish, occasionally used the Danish, Norwegian, Icelandic, and Faroese to denote particular techniques or pattern names. These words have been retained (with the English translation) to give a sense of the original text and to give English-speaking readers a taste of the Scandinavian terms. The pattern instructions have been edited to clarify particular techniques and finishing details. Barbara Liebler and Linda Ligon provided both editing and encouragement, which I greatly appreciate.

My only problem with the book is that I want to knit all the garments, just for me. Long, cold, northern winters would be perfect for making and wearing my Nordic knitting. Someday, perhaps. For now, though, even on the hottest summer days here in Texas, Nordic memories of wild strawberries, the soft sigh of birch leaves in the wind, the green-blue of copper spires, and the icy gray of Baltic waters are all intermingled with my knitting as I hope they will be with yours.

Carol Huebscher Rhoades
Austin, Texas
May 1991

FOREWORD

Time slips by, and the knitter forms stitch after stitch, row after row, in colors and patterns as she pleases. A knitter can knit while the world news flashes by or a passionate drama is played out on the TV screen. Knitting can calm you while you wait for your name to be called in a waiting room or airport. As long as the stitch count is correct and the pattern develops regularly, at least one thing is under control.

Machines produce clothes more cheaply and quickly. But machines can't copy human hand-work or create one-of-a-kind colors and patterns. Machines form stitches evenly and monotonously, with no trace of feeling. Every stitch in a handknitted sweater bears the traces of a time, a trip, a landscape; of persons, events, and thoughts. In many cases, fewer copies of machine-made garments are produced than of home-knitted classics. One such example is the Norwegian Fana sweater, of which hundreds of thousands have been handknitted, if one judges by the number of pattern instructions sold.

This book developed during my travels throughout Scandinavia. People offered me knitting from their private or museum collections; they patiently answered questions, displayed garments, and discussed and gave tips on knitting literature. Some generously lent me old knitting patterns to be reprinted so that many can share them. Without those people, there would have been no book. Others have helped by knitting and writing new instructions based on the old garments. The garments for which instructions are given in this book are not exact copies of traditional clothing but are adaptations, with today's yarns, of simple, useful garments.

I have chosen to show only a small portion of the colors and patterns of the Nordic knitting tradition. Most of the traditional garments represented in this book are festival and holiday clothing, generally made during the nineteenth and twentieth centuries. A few examples of nineteenth-century lace knitting and simple work clothes are included. The sweaters in this book are looser fitting than the original versions, which were styled and fitted differently from today's clothing. Fashion, tradition, personal touches and taste, as well as material and colors, always make their mark on knitting.

The knitting instructions at the end of the book are given to aid those who feel uncertain about knitting a garment on their own. Don't be afraid of the complex patterns and thin needles. You'll find that the color patterning goes smoothly because the sweaters are knit on circular needles—thus all the stitches are knit stitches. Furthermore, it is easier to maintain an even gauge with fine yarn, and the resulting garment will be soft, warm, and pliable. If you're unfamiliar with the basics of knitting, find one of the many excellent beginner books, or even better, an experienced knitter who can teach you.

The garments we have knitted use only pure, natural materials of the highest quality. It is not worthwhile to put so much work into a cheap synthetic yarn which can pill even before the garment is finished.

To give the flavor of the traditional Nordic knitting, we have chosen to knit the new versions in traditional colors and patterns. But there is no limit to the possibilities for those who knit themselves. This is a book of ideas—a pattern collection for inspiration.

Susanne Pagoldh

TECHNIQUE AND STYLE

KNITTING ISN'T DIFFICULT—you just have to know a few basics. All you need are needles and yarn. Needles can be made of old, broken umbrella spokes, a horse's shinbone, reindeer horn, ivory, wood, steel, iron, celluloid, plastic, bamboo, or anything that is sufficiently hard and strong. Traditionally, Nordic garments were knitted in the round with five or more double-pointed needles. The holes for the sleeves were cut open afterward and often edged with woven bands.

We don't know how long women have known how to form stitch after stitch, row after row with needles and a continuous thread. One theory is that knitting came to Europe from the Orient. It is said that the Arabs wore knitted clothing at a very early period, and two pattern-knitted pillow covers which were found in a thirteenth-century royal grave in the province of Burgos in Spain are thought to be of Arabic origin. During the same century, in 1268, the knitters of Paris formed a guild. A fourteenth-century Italian painting showed the Virgin Mary with knitting in her hands, and Bible translations and sermon books from the sixteenth century describe Jesus' clothing as knitted. The first machine for knitting socks was constructed in 1589 by the Englishman William Lee, but it was not until the seventeenth century that machine knitting became common.

Textile techniques similar to knitting existed before and contemporaneously with knitting. *Nålbinding,* which uses a needle with an eye to "sew" the yarn into a tight, inelastic structure, is one such technique that has been known since the Bronze Age. *Nålbinding* mittens were certainly common in Finland and northern Sweden long before the twentieth century.

Knitting's most outstanding feature is its elastic structure. It was quite a while before ribbed cuffs and edgings were developed, however. Old-fashioned stockings and footless leggings (*benholkar,* or "leg nests") had to be tied on with a band under the knee to make them stay up. Now, ribbing is almost synonymous with stockings and leg warmers—our time's *benholkar.*

Woven and sewn clothing came long before

The triangular neck and sleeve gussets are examples of how details from the cutting and fitting of cloth fabric were transferred to knitting. Beside their purely decorative effect, they make a better-fitting garment. Decorative stripes also mark where side and sleeve seams would be, even though the sweater was knit in the round. The sweater comes from Kungshamn in Bohus province and is now in the Nordic Museum in Stockholm. See the full sweater on page 60. Photo: Birgit Brånvall / Nordic Museum.

knitting and were models for it, as shown by the placement of patterns and borders on old garments. Even now, some machine-knitted pantyhose have a seam down the back of the leg. What is now decoration is a reminder of the days when such a feature was necessary.

In the Nordic countries, wool is the most obviously suitable material for knitting, but linen, cotton, silk, horsehair, and human hair have all been used. Throughout history, people have used what was available. When there was a material shortage during the Second World War,

This originally white glove has a cuff 26 cm (10¼ in) long with fringes and borders in two-end knitting. The extremely long fingers are a detail of style which was taken from the gloves worn by the upper classes. Long fingers on a glove indicated that the wearer didn't have to work and instead had servants to perform all practical tasks. The glove shown here was found when the ground was excavated for Copenhagen's city hall in 1892 and is now at the National Museum in Copenhagen. It is difficult to date but it is probably from the seventeenth century. Photo: Lennart Larsen.

celluloid was used. Rayon fibers are derived from wood, but the yarn made from it in earlier times didn't always tolerate water—a thick, fine sweater would shred into bits when it became wet. The textile industry continued to experiment, and other, more water-tolerant, synthetic fibers were developed. Many of these new fibers have disadvantages: for example, acrylic and polyester are petroleum products.

FULLING

One way to make knitted cloth more like fabric is to full it. In the old days, cloth was wetted in warm, soapy water or fish broth and kneaded and rubbed by hand against a wooden washboard. The desired result was a tight, warm cloth in which the stitches could scarcely be distinguished. If you want to full your knitting, choose a yarn which is not made for machine washing, and don't forget to take into account the shrinkage when deciding on gauge and sizing. Be careful about water temperatures: 30° C (86° F) can be just right for some yarns, while others need 60° C (140° F) for proper fulling.

TWO-END KNITTING

Two-end knitting (*tvåändsstickning*) also produces a tight fabric which is very hard-wearing but not very elastic. This old knitting technique was very common in the Dalarna and Jämtland provinces of Sweden but had become almost forgotten. The technique was also common in Norway, Denmark, and Finland, where it was used occasionally for whole garments and sometimes just for decoration or borders.

On the Faroe Islands, people used to wear skølingar when they went out fishing. These knitted and well-fulled outer shoes were reinforced with a wadmal sole and gave a good grip out on the wet, slippery cliffs. These shoes are in the National Museum in Copenhagen. Photo: Niels Elswing.

A new interest in two-end knitting was awakened when a glove from the seventeenth century was found in 1974 at an archaeological site in Falun. When it was compared with knitted examples in the Dalarna Museum and the Nordic Museum, it became apparent that nearly all the knitting from Dalarna had been knitted in the same way as the seventeenth-century glove. This discovery made Birgitta Dandanell and Ulla Danielsson from the Dalarna Museum curious. Together with the handicraft consultant Liv Trotzig, they began research on two-end knitting in 1977. By inventorying and documenting the knitted garments and the knowledge which still remained, they were able to establish the history of two-end knitting in Dalarna, Sweden, and the rest of Scandinavia.

Their research showed that while many knitters still knit stockinette with two ends, very few could knit pattern combinations based on the crook stitch, which is peculiar to two-end knitting and made with one thread in front of and one thread behind the needles, alternating purl and knit stitches. These patterns were knitted in wool, linen, and cotton. When she was young, Elsie Jönsson from Utanmyra on Soller Island saw her grandmother knitting mittens in crook stitches. She still has a linen half mitten made by her grandmother, and she has begun to knit as her grandmother did.

Thanks to Elsie Jönsson and the women at the Dalarna Museum, the techniques for two-end knitting have spread into most areas of the country through books and courses. Elsie leads a couple of courses during the autumn and winter, and now most knitters in the areas around Mora and Soller Island know the art of patterning with two ends. According to Elsie, it is surprisingly easy to do two-end knitting when one has been shown how.

To knit two-ended, hold two strands of yarn in the right hand. Two ends, that is, two threads, are necessary even if the knitting is with one color. If the yarn is wound onto a winding pin (nystpinne), a knife shaft, or a ball winder, it is easy to take one end from the inside and one from the outside of the ball.

To knit stockinette, throw one yarn over the tip of the right needle with the right index finger. For the next stitch, throw the other yarn in the same manner. The threads are alternated (one from the inside of the ball, the next from the outside) with each stitch, twisting around each other in the same direction at all times. This twisting creates a ridged structure on the back which is characteristic of two-end knitting. In certain districts of Norway, it was common to turn two-end knitted mittens inside out and wear them with the ridged side showing.

The bottom section of a two-end-knitted mitten from the Dalarna Museum. The white relief pattern is knitted with crook stitches, a type of patterning possible only in two-end knitting. Notice the decorative red-and-white- and green-and-white-striped purl rows. The mitten was knitted by Elsie Jönsson. The technique is described in Birgitta Dandanell and Ulla Danielsson's book Tvåändsstickat (Twined Knitting, tr. Robin Hansen, Interweave Press). Photo: K. G. Svensson.

It's easy to knit decorative borders with purl stitches in two-end knitting. The stitches are purled and the yarn lies in front of the needles. If dark and light threads are alternated and each thread is twisted at the same place, a diagonal stripe results. Photo: Susanne Pagoldh.

King Charles I of England is said to have worn a light blue silk sweater when he was hanged in 1649. Several silk sweaters in red, yellow, and blue have been preserved in Sweden, Norway, and Denmark. Some of them have star patterns, while others are decorated with magnificent flower and plant motifs. The garment in the picture is from the Historical Museum in Bergen, Norway. Photo: Ann-Mari Olsen/Historical Museum, The University in Bergen.

There are various ways of forming stitches even in conventional knitting. For instance, some knit by throwing the yarn with the right hand, but this is considered to be slower than the method most commonly used in Sweden in which the right hand needle picks up the yarn from the left hand's index finger.

CHANGES IN STYLE

Knitting came to the Nordic countries during the sixteenth and seventeenth centuries, when it was fashionable for the very rich to wear knitted silk stockings and sweaters. Not many could afford to dress so expensively but the common people did copy the patterns, colors, and forms for their own use. Two hundred years later, peasant women in Sweden and Denmark were still wearing similar sweaters, shorter in length and knitted in wool, linen, or cotton, but with the same patterns, colors, and styles as the expensive early silk sweaters.

An example of a detail passed down into folk tradition from the clothing of the upper class is the large cuff on gloves and mittens. In certain areas of Scandinavia, such elaborate cuffs were still knitted and occasionally decorated with fringe and embroidery long after they had fallen out of style among the wealthy, eventually becoming considered as characteristic of the knitting in those particular areas.

A knitting style that was important to knitting in the country cottages was the empire-waisted garment in white cotton. White was the favorite fashion color during the 1700s, and cotton was a new and exciting material, more dazzlingly white than even bleached wool. It was rather expensive at first, but became affordable by the end of that century. Lace patterned gloves, stockings, laces, puffed sleeves, bed covers, and other items were all knitted on sewing-needle-thin needles through the nineteenth century. Bead knitting also became fashionable.

Two hundred years ago, the differences in clothing style between the rich and poor, the upper and middle classes, and city and country dwellers were great. Class distinctions were maintained by royal edicts and laws that decreed who could or could not dress in silk or velvet garments and knitted hose. The only decoration many were allowed was the narrowest silk ribbon.

By the end of the nineteenth century and into the twentieth century, the greatest differences between city and country people had already begun to disappear. At the same time, the middle classes began to be interested in the peasant's traditional clothing, and many museum collections grew with the folk costume movement. Many of the folk costume collections were assembled at that time. Peasant clothes which had previously been regarded as dowdy and unstylish now took on new worth, as did other aspects of the romanticized peasant culture. Traditional knitting patterns also took on new life in sports and outdoor clothing.

PATTERNS

Knitting patterns have been taken from

The Danish woolen lænketrøjen (knitted sweater) from Radbjerg on Falster is an example of how the empire style influenced the length of women's sweaters at the beginning of the nineteenth century. The neck is edged with a silk band. On Falster, the word lænke means "to knit". Compare this sweater with the Danish one on page 22 and the one from Skåne (Sweden) on page 61. This sweater is in the National Museum in Copenhagen. Photo: Niels Elswing.

many different sources. By the sixteenth century, printed pattern books from Germany and Italy were available in Scandinavia. Even though the patterns were originally designed for embroidery in cross stitch or petit point, they were also suitable for knitting. Weaving patterns were also adapted for knitting, although it was most common to copy directly from a colored fabric or a sampler with many patterns knitted in a strip.

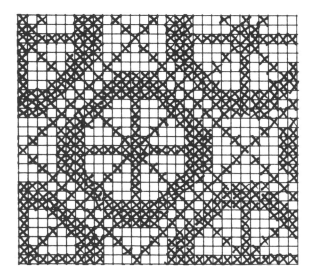

During the nineteenth century, inspiration came from books, newspapers, and fashion magazines which published instructions especially designed for knitting.

Many similar motifs found in knitting came from several parts of the world where they had various symbolic meanings. Often they had religious significance, but it is uncertain if those who knitted them regarded the figures as anything other than decorative.

For example, the eight-pointed star is used in several textile techniques, particularly weaving. It occurs in all the Nordic countries, but in knitted form it is regarded as typically Norwegian. Such stars were knitted and embroidered by the Arabs in Spain during the thirteenth century, and they are seen in the roof carvings of the Moorish palace Alhambra. In Islamic art, the eight-pointed star symbolized the four elements: earth, air, sun, and water, and the qualities of heat, dryness, coolness, and humidity. In Christian art, the eight-pointed star symbolized rebirth. The stars appeared as relief patterns on the expensive silk sweaters imported into Scandinavia during the seventeenth century and are still found on sweaters, mittens, and socks knitted today. The eight-pointed star is based on geometric forms—the

A sun wheel design from a mitten knitted in rust brown and white wool from Tofta on Gotland. The mitten is at the Nordic Museum in Stockholm.

The pattern at the upper left is called tímglasiδ, or hourglass, on the Faroe Islands. To its right is another type of hourglass pattern which was knitted in Norway and Sweden (from Hermanna Stengård's collection at the Gotland Handicraft Shop).

The middle two patterns were knitted on the Faroe Islands. The one on the left is a sun wheel form. Both are constructed by dividing the area with squares and octagons.

In the lower left is a carnation design on a woman's sweater from Halland. The sweater, made in the middle of the eighteenth century, comes from the Årstad district and is now in the Nordic Museum in Stockholm. Next to it is a carnation design from a woman's cap found in a grave on Åland (see page 71).

square and the octagon—which perhaps explains its prevalence. Squares and octagons divide an area evenly, and squares and stripes can be mathematically proportioned.

Another pattern which is common in Nordic knitting is the wheel with spokes. It is a very old symbol, reminiscent of the sun's rays. The hourglass and carnations are also knitted figures with symbolic meaning. The hourglass has been used as a symbol for time and its passage while the carnation has several meanings and has, at various times, symbolized betrothal, divine love, and Christ's death on the cross and his resurrection.

The most important consideration in knitting with two or more colors is that the pattern forms are not spread out over too many stitches; otherwise, the threads on the wrong side become too long and likely to wear poorly or snag. Small, simple lice (seed), square, and diagonal patterns are most suitable and easy to follow. It's easiest to maintain row and stitch gauge if threads are carried over no more than four or five stitches. These strands on the back also form an extra layer of warmth.

DATES AND MONOGRAMS

Considerable labor and care was given to the patterning and color of truly fine clothes. Mittens, stockings, and other garments were often given as presents for weddings and at other festivals. Many of these had the date and initials of the knitter knitted in. Some knitters weren't satisfied with just initials but knitted the whole name or a short text such as "To the Happy Bridal Pair" or similar good wishes.

Dates and initials were also knitted on sweaters, usually in the middle of the chest. Three initials were common in Sweden: one for the first name and two for the family name, which was based on the father's first name and followed by an S for son or a D for daughter. In some districts, such as Delsbo in Hälsingland, four letters were used so that there were the same number of initials as numbers in the date. Occasionally, the letters IHS appeared on fishermen's sweaters. They usually stood for *Iesus Hominum Salvator*,

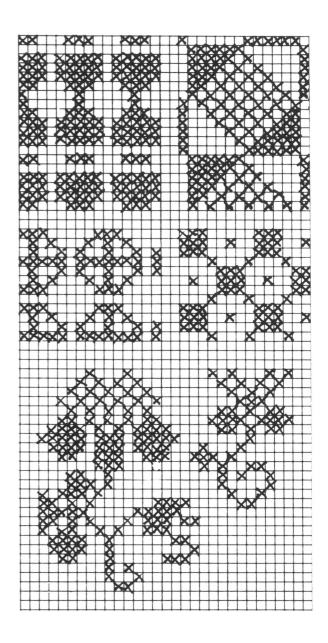

"Jesus, man's savior", or *In Hoc Signo [Vinces]*, "By this sign you shall conquer." In Swedish, the letters also signify *Iesus Herrens Son*, "Jesus, son of the Lord".

COLORS—STRONG AND WEAK

Dyeing has both an expensive and troublesome history. Before synthetic aniline and tar-

Detail from a wool sweater influenced by garments sewn in cloth. The initials and date have been knitted in the chest section. The gauge is more than 40 stitches per 10 cm (4 in). The origin of the sweater is unknown, but it is now in the Historical Museum in Bergen. Photo: Ann-Mari Olsen / Historical Museum, The University in Bergen.

based dyes became readily available at the end of the nineteenth century, only particularly fine cloth was worth dyeing in strong colors. There were exceptions, of course. Even on fine cloth, the dyers were stingy—stocking feet and the bottom portions of sweaters were often left undyed, as it was considered wasteful to dye parts that would be hidden in shoes or trousers.

Simple working or everyday clothes were usually made with undyed yarns or naturally dyed yarns. Heather, tansy, birch, blueberry, woad, weld, and various lichens and mosses all grew near the cottages. Most of the plants yielded weak and transient colors and were not as color-fast as was desirable. Both natural and packet dyes sometimes rubbed off and dyed the skin and other clothes of the wearer and the hands of the knitter.

A dye recipe was found in Cajsa Warg's fa-

mous *Household Hints for Young Women,* published in 1755. This indicates that home dyeing was common at that time, but cloth and yarn were also sent to professional dyers, particularly if one wanted red colors.

Many old sweaters were knitted in undyed, unwashed yarn and dyed afterward. It was thought that cloth processed in this way would be softer. Pattern knitting was often done in white and natural sheep's black; the black took on an even deeper tone when the cloth was dyed red or green. Another advantage to dyeing the cloth afterward was that it was easier to knit with light rather than dark yarn. It takes a strong light and good eyes to knit with black yarn.

Another kind of traditional color effect in yarn was ikat or "flame coloring", a type of tie-dye with yarn. A skein or ball of yarn can be knotted in selected sections before the skein is put into the dyebath. The dye cannot penetrate the places where the yarn is tightly tied, and so those areas remain uncolored. With careful planning, you can space the knots for a desired pattern (zigzag, for example) which will then be revealed as the yarn is knitted. These kinds of patterns were sometimes used on caps from Dalarna or on the Danish *nikulorshuer* (nine-color caps), or were imitated in regular pattern knitting. Another decorative possibility is to knot the skein in so many places that the yarn becomes totally variegated. In stockinette stitch, this yarn gives an irregular salt-and-pepper pattern which was used for indigo blue stockings.

The color blue usually came from indigo, a plant dye which was imported. Nowadays, the color is better known as denim blue and is usually a synthetic dye. It is called *Lodblå,* or pottery blue, in Denmark because it is used to color pots. Processed indigo is placed in a pot with urine, which helps to release the color. Cajsa Warg's recipe recommends using urine from men who have drunk very strong liquor. Other recipes call for urine that is at least six months old. The "naughty pot", as it was called in Denmark, was placed on the chimney block where it was warm and the smell wasn't too disturbing. When the urine had fermented, the garment was placed in the vat and left for several days. Then it was washed thoroughly. Although vat dyeing with indigo was common, it wasn't discussed too loudly. The smell could remain in the garment and make one unpleasant to be around. Sometimes woad or weld, either wild or cultivated, was used for blue colors.

Reds were usually produced with imported materials such as cochineal and madder. Cochineal comes from a little insect which lives on some cactus plants in the Americas. Madder, used to make the color called Turkey red, was both home-grown and imported. Colors from madder vary considerably but are mostly warm red; dyeing at a high temperature yields a rust brown. Various kinds of lichens and Rubiaceae were also used for dyeing reds.

By blending white, black, and brown sheep's wool, you can get shades of gray and light brown.

The art of designing with natural wool colors has been highly developed in Iceland. Even in Norway, a number of traditional patterns are based on natural black or brown and white wools. Natural colors are now in style for knitting, and yarn manufacturers have begun to dye white yarn in shades of natural wool colors.

Detail from an ikat-patterned cotton stocking leg. Flame-patterned knitted stockings were found in several areas of Scandinavia and were even found painted on a eighteenth-century guild chest in Jakobstad's Museum in Finland. The stocking, which is knitted in stockinette with ribbed edges, is in the collection of the Åbo County Museum. Photo: Pekka Kujanpää.

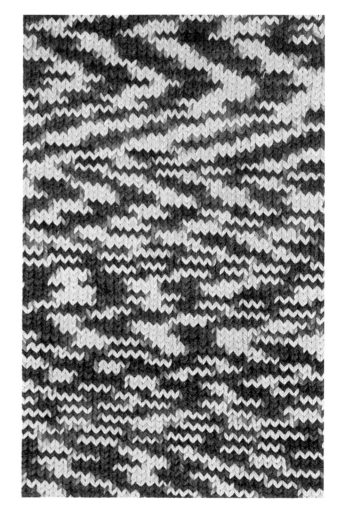

DENMARK

IN A CRYPT in Faarevelje Church on Sjaelland lie the mummified remains of a man. According to legend, he was the Earl of Bothwell, a Scottish nobleman who abducted Queen Mary Stuart and forced her to marry him. He eventually fled Scotland, sailing via the Orkney and Shetland Islands to Bergen and Copenhagen in 1567. He was then arrested and imprisoned in Denmark until his death in 1578. But more interesting than his identity are the knitted stockings he wore for burial.

His grave has been opened and searched three times; Else Ostergård, conservator at the National Museum in Copenhagen, analyzed the fragments of stockings found on the man's legs when the coffin was opened in 1975. If the stockings are as old as researchers believe, then they are the oldest pieces of knitting to be discovered in Denmark. However, the origin of the earl's stockings is unknown.

The top edge of the right stocking is knitted in stockinette stitch with a border of purl-stitch stripes. They are made of a thin, two-ply linen yarn, knitted on very fine needles, used for the thigh-length stockings (*strompehoser*) usually worn by the upper class.

Various tools were used in Danish stocking knitting. The Danish National Museum owns a 19-cm-long, peg-shaped silver knitting tool (a *strikkeske* in Danish or *knytte-pinne* in Skåne dialect) made in the latter half of the sixteenth century. This knitting peg, which belonged to a Danish noblewoman, was used to hold and extend short stocking needles. Needles were held fast against the body by either an arm or a belt, as knitting could proceed more quickly on a stationary needle. Similar knitting pegs have been found elsewhere in Europe.

THE KNITTING INDUSTRY

The center for Denmark's modern textile industry is Herning in Jutland. Hosiery factories are crowded together in the old Jutland *bindeegnen* or knitting district, and many foreign faces are seen in the narrow streets of the city, as buyers, designers, and textile workers from all over the world meet here.

Before the first knitting machines were introduced in Jutland in the middle of the nineteenth century, handknitting provided an essential source of income. On dark winter evenings, young and old gathered for *bindestue* or knitting bees. During the meetings, which lasted until midnight or later, they told stories, sang, and discussed the events of the day while they knitted. A single whale-oil lamp provided lighting for the group. A schoolteacher, Evald Tang Kristenssen, has collected the old knitting songs, and several of them are now included in *Denmark's Old Folk Tunes*.

THIN LITTLE SHEEP

Knitting probably got its start in central Jutland during the famine after the Thirty Years' War (1618–1648). By the middle of the seventeenth century, knitwear was being exported. Small sheep with inferior wool grazed on the unfarmed moors of Jutland. It was said that the sheep were so small, a woman could carry two under each arm. Wool yield in the district was insufficient for the needs of the populace, and additional wool had to be purchased from other

The mittens are based on older examples in the Herning Museum's collection. Note the simple little border on the bottom edge. Pattern, page 112. Photo: Susanne Pagoldh.

areas of the country.

The sheep in south Jutland had long-staple fleeces, and their wool was combed before being spun, whereas that produced in central Jutland was carded. Wool was usually spun on a spinning wheel, although the fishermen on the coast spun yarn for their nets on spindles. The spring wool (*lø*) was separated from the more lustrous summer wool (*uld*). *Skinnull,* wool taken from the sheepskin after slaughtering, shrank considerably.

Dog hair blended with wool strengthened the yarn and was considered a protection against gout. However, dog hair socks were prickly and attracted dogs, which sniffed and sometimes urinated on them. Poor people also collected human hair for blending with wool. Socks and mittens made of dog or human hair blended with wool were popular with the fishermen along the Vester Sea and Lim Fjord. Some fishermen's mittens had two thumbs and were called *stangvantar* (spear mittens) because they were worn when the men speared eels. When one thumb became wet or torn, the mitten could be turned. The two-thumb mittens were also found in many other areas of the Nordic countries.

STOCKING KNITTERS OF THE MOORS

The garments most often knitted were simple, one-color woolen stockings, mittens, sweaters, and underclothing. The men wore knitted underpants, and the women wore knitted underskirts. The quality of these garments was often poor, the stitches still large and loose even after fulling in warm, soapy water or fish broth. After fulling, the cloth was dried on wooden blocks. Stockings were dried on stocking frames so that the shape would be maintained after a shrinkage of approximately 25 percent.

Linen was also used for knitting finer cloth, including stockings. Except in the eastern section, flax was difficult to grow in Jutland, so it was often purchased from areas with better growing conditions.

The hands of the people of Jutland were not allowed to be idle. One had to be doing something

useful every minute. The children of the Jutland moorlands learned to card and spin by the age of five. The men knitted while they rode, plowed, or carried manure; herders knitted while they were out on the moors with the sheep. Women knitted when they worked outside or walked, even while on the way to church on Sundays. Industrious women could knit, ply yarn, churn butter, and rock the baby all at the same time, and some women even knitted while they ate.

The cap in the picture was inspired by a nathue, *or wool nightcap. The original nineteenth-century cap came from Albaek on Jutland and is now in the National Museum in Copenhagen. Kristina Lindkvist wrote the instructions, which are on page 115. Photo: Susanne Pagoldh.*

Detail of a Jutland fisherman's sweater knitted of sheep's wool and woman's hair at a gauge of slightly more than 20 stitches per 10 cm (4 in). The hair blended with wool produces a fabric that is long-wearing and a good protection against moisture. The sweater is in the Herning Museum. Photo: Kjeld Hansen/Herning Museum.

Using the wool / hair-blend fisherman's sweater from the Herning Museum as a model, Carina Pagoldh has designed a pattern for a new sweater which is considerably wider than the original. In this example, hair was blended with unbleached, combed flax, and spun into a thin, uneven thread. Your own hair, dog hair, or any other fiber can be combined with wool. Pattern on page 91. Photo: Susanne Pagoldh.

The yarn ball would be fastened onto a hook hanging from the knitter's shoulder or set in a bowl and then pulled from the inside of the ball so that it wouldn't roll around. Sometimes, the yarn was wound onto the dried windpipe of a goose which had been filled with peas or pebbles and closed into a ring. The mistress could tell by the rattling of the peas whether or not the maid was doing her work properly.

Knitting in Jutland was done "citywise" (*bymåde*), the yarn being picked up from the fingers of the left hand. This method used by women in the cities was considered finer and quicker than *bondemåden,* the method practiced by the peasants in other parts of Denmark in which the yarn was thrown onto the point of the right needle with the help of the right-hand fingers.

FOOTLESS STOCKINGS

It has been said that the Jutland stocking knitters whose work warmed so many other feet went barefoot in the summers and wore footless stockings with clogs during the grim, snowy winters on the moors. These footless stockings, with such names as: *stunthoser, stomper, stomphoser,* and *pløjser,* were commonly worn by both men and women in Jutland until the Second World War. As with medieval hose, the stocking shafts were held by straps or bands around the foot.

In 1636, Christian IV decreed that wives in Holstein and South Jutland were under no circumstances to wear knitted stockings. We can infer from this that stockings were still considered at that time to be part of the dress of the higher class. Silk and velvet were also fabrics to be worn only by royalty and members of the nobility. The status of a man could be determined by his footwear: long stockings were considered finer than short socks. Also, more work was involved, and more money was paid for men's stockings, which were displayed below the knee breeches, than for women's stockings, hidden by long skirts.

Life in the knitting districts has been described in several stories by Steen Steensen. The best known is "E. Bindstouw", written in 1842. In one of his stories, the term *stundthosetøs* (footless stockings) is used to disparage a woman character.

Another story has been passed down about the author Søren Kierkegaard who was nicknamed Søren Sok (Sock) because he always wore clothing of heavy cloth, woolen stockings, and shoes instead of boots. The name also mocked the background of his father, who had been a *hosekræmmer,* or stocking tradesman, from West Jutland before he became a wealthy manufacturer in Copenhagen.

The Jutland stocking sellers wandered from farm to farm with their wares. The cleverest salesmen would take an old, torn sweater as part payment for a new one and then sell the old sweater at the next farm. By 1691, complaints were made against the Jutland stocking sellers who swarmed Amager Square. Their wares were originally all handknitted, but in time, the larger portion of their assortment was machine knitted.

A pløjs or footless stocking and a "spear mitten" with two thumbs. These pieces, both from the beginning of the twentieth century, are in the Herning Museum. Photo: Kjeld Hansen / Herning Museum.

In spite of little or no education, many of these stocking sellers ended up as well-situated manufacturers or hosiery factory owners.

WARM HEADS

The people of Jutland may have had cold feet but they had warm heads. The *nathue,* a red knitted nightcap, was worn daily by most of the peasant men from the 1700s until the middle of the nineteenth century. It was then restyled into a peaked cap.

The knitted caps could be worn doubled. Sometimes these caps had pile linings, or they might have a red or blue turned-up pile brim. The lining was most often knitted in unbleached white yarn to conserve colored yarn. A distinctive house cap, knitted in white cotton or wool yarn, was worn indoors.

Some long, colorfully patterned double caps have been preserved in several Danish museums. The *nikulørshuer* or nine-color caps were worn by farmers from the islands south of Fyn. The caps are patterned in four or five colors, not in nine as the name implies. One theory suggests that the name comes from *ny,* new, and signifies new colors.

Most caps are similar in style and color. Motifs were made by common two-color pattern knitting or by the use of ikat or tie-dyed yarns. Careful preparation was needed in knotting the yarn skeins before dyeing to obtain the desired patterns. An ikat-patterned cap at the National Museum in Copenhagen is so finely and evenly knitted that it seems machine made. Long caps (*luvor*) with tie-dyed patterns have also been knitted in the Dalarna area of Sweden.

MEN'S SWEATERS

Tie-dyed color patterns were also used on knitted sleeves which were sewn onto the body of a woven sweater or vest. When the body was woven in checks and the knitted sleeves had tie-dye patterns, the result was truly striking. More commonly, blue- or white-striped sleeves were sewn onto a white, undyed wadmal body or blue-and-white-striped undershirts were worn under a vest. Men's sweaters patterned with eight-pointed stars in blue and white come from Sejero, an island off the coast of Sjaelland.

NIGHTSHIRTS

A knitted, tight-fitting nightshirt was part of the women's costumes in Denmark, the districts of Skåne and Halland in Sweden, and parts of Norway. The shirt was worn during the day as a kind of undershirt under a cloth bodice, with the sleeves the most visible part of the garment.

In south Falster, in Amager and Rosnaes, the sleeves were normally sewn directly onto a cloth

A nikulørshue (nine-color cap) from Svendborg on Fyn. The plain part is turned inside the patterned area as a lining so that the cap is doubled. Such caps have been knitted since the nineteenth century with either ikat-dyed yarn or, as shown here, with color changes in common two-color pattern knitting. The cap is in the National Museum in Copenhagen. Photo: Niels Elswing.

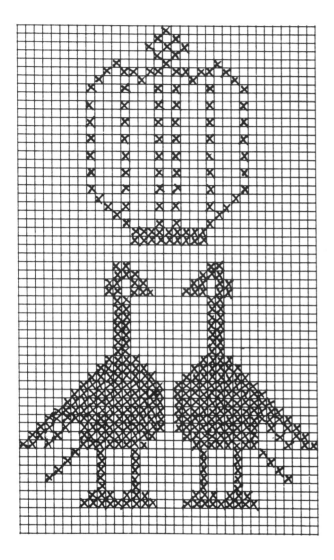

The flower and animal motifs in this diagram are characteristic of the knitting from Amager. The patterns are created with purl stitches on stockinette. The birds are on black knitted sleeves from the latter half of the nineteenth century. The bird cage is drawn from a red knitted shawl. The pieces are in the National Museum in Copenhagen.

Detail of a nightshirt in the Herning Museum. The shirt, dated from the end of the eighteenth century, is regarded as one of the oldest in Denmark. Note the borders in two-end knitting around the neck and on the lower edge of the sleeve. The wool fabric is knitted at a gauge of slightly more than 40 stitches per 10 cm (4 in). Photo: Kjeld Hansen/Herning Museum.

bodice. Patterns on the Dutch Amager woman's sweater sleeves were knitted in black with large, coiling animal, flower, and star motifs made of purl stitches on a stockinette ground. The Amager Dutch had enjoyed special privileges since the time of Christian II (1520s) because they supplied Copenhagen Castle with onions and root vegetables. Perhaps because of their privileged status, they considered it dishonorable to knit. It has been theorized that Swedes from Halland or Skåne knitted the sweaters found in Amager.

Most of the nightshirts preserved in Danish museums are red, green, black, or blue with patterns in damask knitting—relief patterns made with purl stitches on a stockinette ground. Eight-

pointed stars within diagonal squares were very common. This type of pattern is found on an exquisite silk shirt from the seventeenth century (see photo, page 11).

The length of the nightshirts was determined by the whims of fashion. The longest shirts are considered the oldest, and shirts that ended just below the breast (see page 12) came into fashion at the beginning of the nineteenth century. Some of the shirts had pile borders or cloth bands and edgings which were sewn on.

The majority of the women's shirts were knitted on circular needles. The lower edges were patterned with checkerboard squares or diagonal lines to counteract the tendency of the edge to roll up. Increases and decreases in the body and sleeves could be made within the pattern by careful counting so that the size of the stars and squares gradually increased. Borders in two-end knitting were also common. These shirts were often knitted in white unbleached yarn and dyed afterward.

It is not easy to knit a nightshirt. The pat-terns, which require careful counting, are most effectively knitted with a thin yarn on fine needles. Very complicated patterns with *drejede,* or twisted stitches, were knitted on Falster. Ironically, many of these professionally knitted shirts were mended very clumsily by their less talented owners.

Using the red night-shirt in the Herning Museum as a model, Kristina Lindkvist has knitted a new shirt, like the original but with wider sleeves. Using a thicker, softer yarn produced a looser fabric with enlarged patterns. Two-end knitting with purl stitches was used on the borders, but one could also knit them with the common two-thread technique. The diagonal pattern on the body's lower edge not only is decorative but prevents the edge from rolling back on itself. Pattern on page 107. Photo: Susanne Pagoldh.

THE FAROE ISLANDS

ACCORDING TO AN old saying, "Sheep's wool is Faroese gold." As far back as the old Faroese sagas, people talked of the trading between Norway and the Faroe Islands: Faroese wool and woolen goods were exchanged for timber to build houses and boats. The islands are spread out halfway between Scotland and Iceland and are devoid of bushes and trees because the Atlantic winds sweep over the green mountainsides. However, the Gulf Stream keeps the climate mild, damp, and changeable. Faroese, a west Nordic language related to Icelandic and Danish, is spoken there. The island group belongs to Denmark but has a degree of self-government.

It is not known how long people have knitted on the Faroes, but by the end of the sixteenth century, knitted stockings were being exported to Norway. During the next century, knitting as an export increased so much that knitted stockings and fishermen's sweaters became the Faroes' most important export goods. For example, in 1765, about 100,000 pairs of stockings were exported. Men carded and spun the wool, at first with spindles and later with hand-driven spinning wheels. The women wove and knitted.

FISHERMEN'S SWEATERS

When Susanna Johansen of Strendor, who was born and raised in Lamba on Eysturoy, was seven years old in 1906, she and her grandmother knitted *skibstroyggjur*, fishermen's sweaters, to sell. Every day, Susanna had to knit her rows before she was allowed to go out and play. Susanna and her grandmother knitted the body of the sweater together. They sat opposite one another and knitted around on 8 to 12 double-pointed needles, depending on how large the sweater was to be. The yarn was held in the right hand, in typical Faroese fashion. The sleeves were knitted from the top down to the cuffs, which were bound off without ribbing. The armhole was cut open and the sleeves sewn in. The hole for the neck was only a slit with no finishing other than binding off.

The work had to go as quickly as possible, so only simple patterns such as *Støra* and *Lítla skák* (long and short slants), *Skák og teinur* (slants and sticks), and *Loppan* (lice) were knitted. The small, closely spaced patterns made the garment elastic, and an extra layer was formed on the inside by the threads which were carried so short a distance that they didn't need to be twisted or caught up.

The yarns were thick and gray or dyed aniline red, although the bottom part of the garments was often knitted with natural white yarn. The red color was called *korki* after a lichen which was used for dyeing before synthetic colors became available at the end of the nineteenth century. The lichen *korki* gives a blue-red color which can range from rose pink and light purple to dark wine red.

Sweaters similar to those exported from the Faroes have also been knitted in Halland, Sweden. Faroese-type patterns called *jyske* (which means that they are regarded as coming from Jutland) are found in southern Halland. Such sweaters have also been dubbed Icelandic, but it isn't true that the pattern is knitted in Iceland. Similar sweaters are seen in photographs from turn-of-the-century Greenland, and according to the price list at the Royal Greenland Store, the sweaters were imported from Jutland and the Faroe Islands.

The yarn used for the fishermen's sweaters was thick and hard and spun mostly from the sheep's outer coat of long, thick hairs. Yarn spun from the short, soft undercoat (*nappa togv*) was used only for the family's better clothes. The labor

A view of the islands of Hestur and Koltur from Velbastadur on Streymoy. Photo: Susanne Pagoldh.

Long slants and sticks is a common pattern on Faroese fishermen's sweaters.

of plucking the down from the hair was so time-consuming that it could take three days to get the wool for one jacket. For a really fine Sunday jacket, a dark brown down wool was used. The Faroese author Jens Christian Svabo, who traveled around the islands in 1781 and 1782, reported that up to l kilo (2.2 pounds) could be spun in one day and that two knitters working together could knit 1½ sweaters per day. When the sweaters were finished, they were taken to shops in the village and sold to merchants. Payment was usually in goods, and those who didn't have their own wool had to knit three sweaters to get paid for one. The work, which involved not only knitting but carding, spinning, and washing, was so demanding that every minute of spare time was used for it. Milkmaids knitted on the way to and from the milking.

Between Christmas and New Year's Day, no knitting was done for the men, according to Susanna Johansen. Anyone who went out fishing in a sweater knitted during that period would not come back. But it was all right to knit garments to sell.

SHOES AND STOCKINGS

When Susanna was young and went to the fells with the cows, she usually wore *leggold*, footless leggings which covered the lower leg. Both inside and outside the house, she also wore *skóleistur*, short double-knitted and fulled socks. These are still knitted and are worn like slippers.

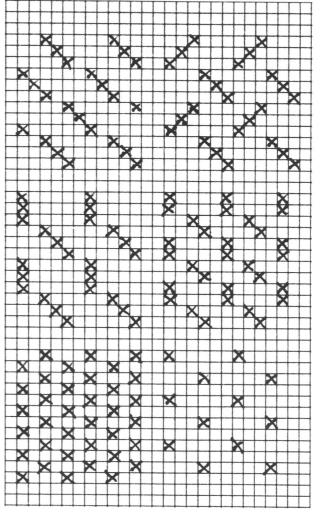

Skóleistur knitted by Nicolina Jensen from a Sørvåg pattern (instructions, page 115). Photo: Susanne Pagoldh.

Sweaters for export had simple patterns such as long slants, long slants back and forth, long slants and sticks, and short slants and sticks (see page 24). Loppan, (lice) and Pikkini ("pecking with a bird's beak") are at right and left at the bottom of the chart.

This nineteenth century konufólka-troyggja from the Torshavn Museum has more than 60 stitches and 70 rows per 10 cm (4 in)! Photo: Nicolina Jensen.

This sweater is knitted in a softer and finer yarn than the heavy sweaters previously knitted for export. The pattern is called Gásaryggur, gooseback. Instructions are on page 85. Photo: Susanne Pagoldh.

which came up over the knees, and soft skin shoes. *Skølingar,* a type of knitted and well-fulled outer shoe with a sole of heavy felted fabric, were worn over the skin shoes (see p. 9). The *skølingar* made it easier to walk on the wet cliffs without slipping, and both they and *skóleistur* were also worn in the fells.

NATIONAL COSTUME

The thick, natural-colored sweaters which are now knitted in the Faroe Islands and sold to tourists were previously worn only by men and boys while working or at sea. In the old days, men who worked in the towns wore a woven wool vest over a blue-and-white knitted undersweater similar to Danish striped undersweaters or Norwegian Fana sweaters (see page 43). These undersweaters were sometimes edged with red woven bands or cloth strips; they were worn up until the beginning of the twentieth century.

Another part of the men's national costume is the *knappatroyggja,* a knitted jacket patterned in light and dark blue and edged with red bands. Twelve red-bordered buttonholes and twelve silver or tin buttons lined the front opening. The jacket is still worn with an embroidered vest, black wadmal (felted fabric) knee pants, and knitted stockings for festivals such as weddings or national holidays. Men also wore *frynsamuffur,* knitted wrist warmers which were embroidered and had fringe sticking out at the wrist.

Konufólkatroyggja, short-sleeved, pattern-knitted bodices were part of the women's national costume. Four colors are traditional: red, blue, green, and white. Older women and those in mourning wore bodices knitted in dark and light blue, and never in red. Now the bodices are often knitted in red and dark blue with thin yarn and fine needles. The old patterns were often named after the knitter who first created the pattern. One pattern which has been preserved is the eight-pointed star in a diagonal box.

A woven striped skirt was worn with the bodice. It was said that when a woman got a skirt, a man got a cap. A piece of the striped fabric was cut out from the skirt's front section and replaced

The men who went out to sea needed several changes of sweaters, mittens, and stockings. A fishing expedition to Iceland lasted two months and required four changes of clothes. A trip to Greenland lasted four months and needed seven changes. Even into the 1920s, some men who fished in small open boats were clothed in the traditional fisherman's costume of sewn hide and three-quarter-length trousers worn over wool clothes. They wore knitted stockings, *pulshosur,*

with cloth of lesser quality, which wasn't visible under the apron. One still sees men in Torshavn wearing red-and-blue striped cloth caps with twelve folds in the top which protect the wearer against the trolls.

WOMEN'S SHAWLS

On the Faroes, the triangular knitted shawl is called *bundnaturriklæðið*. It is uncertain whether the name comes from *binda,* to knit, or from the fact that the shawl is worn bound at the back. The name could also refer to an old technique of tying the shawl onto a triangular board with nails.

Triangular shawls have been knitted in several Nordic countries, and they have been knitted in the Faroe Islands at least since the end of the nineteenth century. They are still popular among young women. They are distinguished from those knitted in Norway by the extra gore in the center which makes them four-edged. The gore narrows towards the upper edge so that the shawl fits well around the shoulders. The shawl's ends are long enough that they can be crossed over the chest, wrapped around the back, and then brought back to the front and tied at the waist. The shawls were also large enough to draw over the head during bad weather.

Shawls are knitted in natural colors, usually in one color with a lace border or with one or more borders in various colors. Traditionally, most shawls were knitted with only a simple crocheted edge rather than a fringe. The finer shawls knitted with thin yarn often had fringe and were lined in white so that the lace pattern would show up clearly.

DEBES'S PATTERN BOOK

As the nineteenth century ended, contacts with the outer world increased, and interest in the national costume and old patterns were almost forgotten. Patterned sweaters were replaced with solid-colored dark blue or dark brown ones. However, some people still interested in handicrafts organized several exhibits, and a number of the old knitting patterns were collected and knitted up in a long sampler which was shown in Copenhagen in 1929. The Danish queen Alexandrina was so charmed by the patterns that she gave the master tailor Hans Marius Debes the mission of collecting and publishing a book of Faroese knitting patterns. *Føroysk bindingarmynstur* by Debes, published in 1932, listed more than 100 patterns which are still knitted today, and the book has been reprinted by Heimavirki, the handicraft center in Torshavn.

Many older women continue to knit shawls, mittens, sweaters, and *skóleistur* to sell, although they earn very little. The fishermen's sweaters are knitted by hand in simple patterns because it is too difficult to knit tight, complicated patterns in heavy yarn. More intricately patterned sweaters knitted with thin yarn are usually done by machine with pattern cards. These are exported worldwide.

Susanna Johansen still knits, mostly for her own family. Susanna's daughter, Nicolina Jensen, continues the tradition. For the past fifteen years, she has taught courses on the old Faroese wool crafts, including spinning, and she helps with the textile collection in the Torshavn Museum.

Frynsamuffur *(at left), knitted and embroidered wool wrist warmers from the Torshavn Museum collection. Photo: Susanne Pagoldh.*

The instructions for the shawl Jóhanna Maria *comes from the Faroese Handicraft Center. It can be knitted in either a one- or two-ply yarn. Instructions, page 110. Photo: Susanne Pagoldh.*

GREENLAND

GREENLAND IS AN immense island, the world's largest, which lies in the waters between Europe and North America. It is a continent, almost entirely covered with glaciers, a neighbor of Canada, close to the North Pole, and populated by Greenlanders and Danes. The island was a Danish colony for 250 years, and even though it still belongs to Denmark, it has some degree of self-government. The languages spoken there are Danish and Greenlandic, an Eskimo language.

Greenland's knitting tradition is rather young. Mariane Petersen of the National Museum in Nuuk (Godthåb) believes that mitten knitting began some time during the 1850s. Traditionally, skin mittens were worn. Greenland's women learned to knit from Danish women when they worked for them as maids. Imported yarn was purchased in the Danish-controlled shops.

Hares were large and plentiful on Greenland, so their fiber was used as well as sheep's wool. Clothes knitted with hare yarn are unbelievably smooth and pleasant against the skin. Usually the hare fiber was spun on a spindle. Mariane Petersen's grandfather (born in 1863) was a hunter in Kangamiut and Manitsok (Sukkertoppen) on the west coast, and he wore caps and mittens knitted with soft white hare fiber. A hunter wearing white clothing while out in his kayak was scarcely visible against the ice.

Dogs also have soft, fine hair which is easy to spin, and sweaters are still knitted with it. Garments knitted with dog hair are soft and nice but not as strong as those knitted with sheep's wool.

Mariane also notes that in the northern parts of Greenland, fox fur was spun and knitted. Arctic foxes can be white or blue.

SHEEP BREEDING

Erik the Red and other Vikings from Iceland came to Greenland before A.D. 1000, bringing domesticated animals, including sheep, with them. About 500 years later, the Norsemen and their animals had disappeared from Greenland—no one knows how or why. In 1721, Hans Egede, a citizen of the Danish-Norwegian kingdom, sailed from Bergen to look for the Norsemen and to Christianize the natives. Sheep were among the necessities shipped to the colony by Hans Egede.

It wasn't until 1906, when the Reverend Jens Chemnitz brought in twelve sheep from the Faroe Islands, that sheep breeding was seriously begun on Greenland. Some years later, sheep were imported from Iceland and a royal sheep station was started in Qaqortoq (Julianehåb) in southern Greenland. Today's Greenland sheep are descendants of those Icelandic and Faroese sheep.

In the southern part of the continent, the summer months are warm and grass is plentiful. During mild winters, the temperature can stay above 10° C (50° F), and the sheep can graze in snow-free areas. Other winters are grim with heavy snowfalls and sudden polar winds. For example, in 1966 the temperature dropped to −43° C (−45° F) on the first of January. More than 20,000 out of 40,000 sheep died. The latest catastrophic winter was in 1975, when about 5000 sheep died.

Since then, sheep have been kept in during winter snows. There are very few trees on Greenland, and so most building materials are imported. Because of this, sheep are sometimes sheltered in unusual places, like the barracks of an American military base.

Today, there are more than 20,000 sheep. There would be pasture for considerably more, but the hay must be saved for winter fodder. Sheep are also given fish meal during the winter for extra nutrition.

Because of the harsh climate, the outer hair of the sheep has become long and lustrous, while the undercoat is soft and fine. Inner and outer coats are spun together for a strong and soft yarn suitable for knitting. The sheep are shorn in June. A better-quality wool would be obtained if the sheep were shorn in May, but that is considered too risky. Sheep need to eat four times as much to hold in body warmth after shearing. The wool from Greenland's sheep is washed and spun in Denmark, but Greenland plans on having its own wool-processing facilities within the next year.

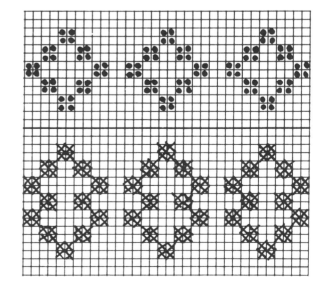

The sweater at right was knitted during the 1950s in Igaliko in southern Greenland. The pattern forms are similar to the skin embroideries which were sewn onto kamikker, *the traditional Greenland women's boots. Instructions for the sweater are on page 85. From Gudrun Chemnitz's collection in Nuuk. Photo: Marie Nilsson.*

A MIXED TRADITION

On Greenland, knitting is done in the Danish way—the yarn is held in the left hand—according to Gudrun Chemnitz, a consultant from Greenland's Women's Union Collection in Nuuk and granddaughter of Jens Chemnitz, one of Greenland's first sheep raisers. In 1915, a Miss Lindahl came from Iceland to teach Greenlanders about sheep-raising methods. She brought a spinning wheel with her and also taught the residents how to card, spin, and knit. One of the pupils was Gudrun's mother, Magga. Later on, Magga also became a teacher.

Homemaking courses were one of the few educational opportunities for Greenland's women during the first half of this century. Women learned Danish cooking and handwork in these schools. Gudrun, who attended one of them, says that knitting was one of the handicrafts taught.

Greenland's knitters don't usually use instructions. The first instruction booklet came out in 1983, when Gudrun translated an Icelandic pattern for the women's college. "Patterns should come from one's head," they say, but many knitters do work from pictures in Danish and other foreign weekly magazines.

Another source of inspiration for Greenland's knitters is the fisherman's sweater. There are many turn-of-the-century photographs of fishermen and Greenlanders dressed in sweaters patterned with designs from Debes's Faroese pattern book. The slant and stick pattern (see pages 24 and 39) was particularly common in the pictures. Although the sweaters are referred to as "Icelandic", the old price lists from the Danish shops show that the sweaters were imported from Jutland and the Faroe Islands.

Gudrun has collected knitted pieces for many years. The oldest sweater in her collection was knitted during the 1920s; it was knitted back and forth on straight needles and patterned with several colors. She says that circular needles didn't come to Greenland until just after the Second World War. All of her sweaters are from southern Greenland and were knitted with local wool in natural colors. She says that more brightly col-

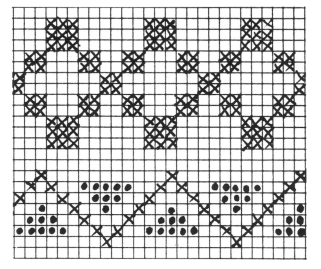

Patterns drawn from wool sweaters in Gudrun Chemnitz's collection.

The cap is knitted back and forth on two needles and the edges sewn together into a tube. The little tufted button at the top of the cap is knotted. Persida Lund from Nuuk says that such caps were certainly worn by dog sled drivers in northern Greenland. Her grandfather, who was born in 1880, wore a similar cap and black-and-white-striped wrist warmers when he hunted or fished. The cap is in a private collection in Nuuk. Photo: Marie Nilsson.

The sweater at left was bought in Igalike in southern Greenland sometime during the 1920s. Between the pattern rows are stripes 5 cm (2 in) wide in salt-and-pepper yarn. Instructions for this sweater of Greenland wool yarn are on page 85. From Gudrun Chemnitz's collection. Photo: Marie Nilsson.

These silky-smooth mittens were knitted in Nûgâtsiaq in northern Greenland. The yarn was spindle-spun with clean white hare fiber. The mittens are in Gudrun Chemnitz's collection in Nuuk. photo: Marie Nilsson.

ored yarns were always bought. Although the leather which decorated the *kamikkerna,* Greenland's traditional soft skin boots, was dyed with lichens and birch leaves, Gudrun doesn't remember ever hearing about yarn being dyed.

The colors, patterns, and designs of the Greenland sweaters are reminiscent of those from the Faroe Islands. But they also have a Greenlandic character: the patterns made up of squares are very similar to the embroidered skin pieces sewn onto women's *kamikker.*

The only knitted part of Greenland's national costume was a cap. Photographs from about the time of the First World War up until the 1950s show all the women with caps as part of their costume. Similar caps have also been worn by men for hunting or fishing.

Interest in knitting has increased during the past few years, says Gudrun. There is a great desire for experimentation, and even spinning and knitting with polar bear fur have been tried! Musk ox wool is popular for children's sweaters, but it is difficult to come by. The luster of the outer coat of the musk ox is like that of human hair, but it is softer. The women's union has given courses in knitting and dyeing, and it sponsored a contest for collecting Greenland patterns. It is hoped that eventually sweaters knitted with Greenland's wool will be available for export and tourist sales.

BEADING

Whether Greenland's beaded collars were the inspiration for the Norwegian and Icelandic circular knitted sweaters (page 40) has been a subject of dispute. In any case, there is a definite relation between the beaded and knitted patterns and pattern placement on garments. The style gained significance when the Danish royal couple were photographed in Greenland costumes after their visit in 1952.

Beads have been a form of hard currency on Greenland for more than 200 years. During the seventeenth century, many whaling ships came to Greenland from Holland carrying milk white or blue beads from Amsterdam. The whalers traded the beads, called *sapanngat* or glass corals, for sealskins, blubber, and whale oil. But beads were found in Greenland long before the Europeans came with their glass corals. Beads which could be dyed with blood were made from bone, stone, and the teeth or backbones of a certain little fish. Anything with a hole in it was considered a beneficial female fertility symbol, and beads were often worn hidden as a source of protection.

As time went on, beads were easier to obtain, and the decorations on women's costumes became larger and heavier. Wood carvings from the middle of the nineteenth century show Greenlanders with beaded collars that barely reached below the shoulders. By the turn of the century, beaded collars had grown so much that they went half way down to the elbows.

A large beaded collar could weigh 1.5 kilos (3.3 pounds) and contain as many as 30,000 small glass beads. The collars are not knitted but are made of beads sewn onto a net backing. The technique is not unique to Greenland; similar beadwork has been found in other parts of the world, such as Africa and Mongolia.

Beaded wrist warmers, called *tajarutit*, were knitted in wool. These wrist warmers, which are part of the national costume, originally came from Denmark sometime during the nineteenth century. Wrist warmers similar to those found on Greenland are also preserved in several muse-

These red wrist warmers from western Greenland were found in a box at the National Museum in Copenhagen in 1984. It is not known how old they are, but interest in them has recently awakened. Photo: Lennart Larsen.

ums in Scandinavia. Knitting with beads threaded onto yarn was popular in Europe during the Empire period at the beginning of the nineteenth century.

Older wrist warmers from Greenland vary considerably in colors and patterns. Nowadays, the most common ones have white beads on a red ground for younger women and white beads on a blue ground for older ones. Patterns are designed by the knitter. Wrist warmers can also be knitted in striped patterns without beads or lengthened so that they go up to the elbow. Beaded wrist warmers are not knitted for men, but simple ones in undyed yarn are welcome presents for hunters, who wear them underneath skin mittens.

Wrist warmers are the only knitted garments which are part of the national costume. Beads are threaded onto yarn before knitting. Instructions for the beaded wrist warmers are on page 114. Photo: Susanne Pagoldh.

The beaded collars of Greenland may have inspired the method for knitting patterns around the sweater yokes on circular needles with decreases evenly spaced in rows. The collars have strong similarities to patterns and placement used on Norwegian and Icelandic sweaters (see page 41). For the Greenland collars, beads are threaded onto a string and then sewn onto netting. This costume belongs to the collection of the Greenland Women's Union in Nuuk. Photo: Marie Nilsson.

ICELAND

THE FIRST NORDIC settlers came to Iceland from Norway sometime during the ninth century. They crossed the Atlantic in open boats, bringing sheep and other domesticated animals with them. Trade in sheep, wool, and woolen goods has been lively since that time. The sagas were written in Icelandic, a west Nordic language which has retained many old forms.

The oldest piece of knitting found in Iceland is a simply knitted wool mitten dating from the first half of the sixteenth century. The mitten was found at an archaeological site at Storaborg in southern Iceland. The first Icelandic Bible, printed in 1584, confirms that knitting was a well-known technique by that time. The account books of the Bible's translator, the Bishop of Holar, show that knitted garments were used as a medium of exchange as early as 1582. There are theories that knitting was introduced by either English, Dutch, or German merchants, but no one knows how or when this might have happened.

A great deal of knitting was done both for home use and export. As early as 1624, about 72,000 pairs of stockings and 12,000 pairs of mittens were being exported. Both men and women knitted. The men carded and combed the wool while the women spun it, at first on spindles, and by the end of the eighteenth century, on spinning wheels. Sometimes yarn was skeined onto a sheep bone. On dark winter evenings, everyone gathered in the baðstofa, or sitting room, to work together and listen to the old sagas being read aloud. These evenings in the baðstofa also functioned as school time when the children could learn how to read.

"After you are four years old, you should begin to work. Three arts shall you learn: reading, spinning, and knitting." This free translation from an old folk song meant that children had knitting in their hands from a very early age, but normally, they didn't have to knit a certain amount per week until they were eight years old.

Two pairs of fishermen's mittens a week were considered enough for a child. A maidservant was expected to turn out a pair of long stockings a day, but she was allowed to work undisturbed on them. Two maids working together could produce four sweaters a week. They often sat opposite one another and knitted around on the same sweater body. Garments were fulled after knitting. During the weeks before Christmas, the work in the baðstofa went furiously because everyone had to get new clothes for Christmas. Those who didn't have any would be eaten up by the Christmas cat, a large and dangerous animal described in the sagas.

The coast near Akranes, a few miles north of Reykjavik on Iceland's west coast. Photo: Marie Nilsson.

Roðskor, soft shoes sewn of fish skin, which used to be worn in the area of the western fjords. The shoe in the picture is sewn of wolffish skin. Both it and the knitted sole are in the National Museum in Reykjavik (nr. 1965:116 and 1963:385). Photo: Susanne Pagoldh.

Most knitters worked in the round on five or more needles. Needles not being used were kept in wooden boxes called *prjónastokkur.* The boxes were usually carved with the owner's name and a date and occasionally with a verse or scroll pattern.

NOT ONLY SHEEP'S COLORS

In *A Trip Through Iceland,* published in 1772, the Icelandic skald, or historian, Eggert Olafsen, remarks that farmers wore black clothes so that they could contemplate life's sorrows and that they wore knitted underclothes and stockings.

Laufaviδarvett-lingar, mittens which have been knitted in the western fjord country since the middle of the nineteenth century. The mitten belongs to the Icelandic Handicraft Union in Reykjavik. Below is a diagram of the pattern. Photo: Susanne Pagoldh.

(far left) This unusually gaudy wool mitten has cross-stitch embroidery and is more than 100 years old. It was knitted for a woman's hand and is similar to most of the two-thumb Icelandic mittens. A text which cannot be translated is embroidered on the lower edge. National Museum in Reykjavik. Photo: Susanne Pagoldh.

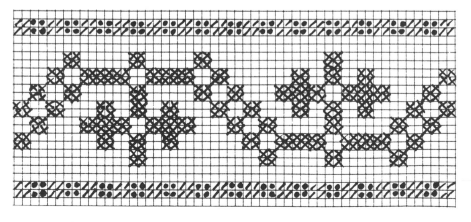

Lace-knitted wool handstúkur, or wrist warmers, worn by both men and women. The pattern is called krónuprjón (crown knitting) or rósastrengsprjón (rose-path knitting). Elsa E. Guðjónsson has written the instructions on page 115 using a pair from the early twentieth century as a model. Photo: Susanne Pagoldh.

Most knitting was done with natural-colored yarns, but those who had the means decorated finer clothing with embroidery and dyed yarns. Those who were well off wore clothes of foreign materials such as silk and velvet. Silk stockings were common.

There are eight pattern books with hand-drawn graphs for embroidery or weaving in the National Museum in Reykjavik. The oldest book is from the seventeenth century. In two of the eight books, the patterns are also suitable for knitting. Three patterns in a book from 1776 seem to be for knitting *brjóstadúkar,* men's vests. Although no pattern-knitted vests have been preserved, it has been assumed that they were knitted in several colors, according to Elsa E. Guðjónsson, director for the textile division of Iceland's National Museum.

It is uncertain how the sweaters knitted for export really looked. Not a single one remains. Elsa Guðjónsson suggests that they were knitted simply in stockinette stitch with one color. Old photographs sometimes show Icelandic men wearing single-color sweaters that have ribbing as the only embellishment. Although the slant and stick pattern (see picture, page 24) has sometimes been connected with Iceland by other Scandinavians, Elsa is uncertain whether it was actually knitted there. It is possible that the Icelandic sweaters got their name from the Icelandic wool.

MITTENS WITH TWO THUMBS

Pattern-knitted mittens from the western fjords are called *laufaviðarvettlingar,* ("leafy-wood mittens") which evokes vegetation, trees, and leaves. Both dyed and undyed yarns were used in the wavy patterns which are similar to those in the old pattern books.

Sigríður Halldórsdóttir, rector of the handicraft school in Reykjavik, reports that sailors' mittens had a cross on them for protection while they were at sea. Wavy patterns have been used for mittens since the middle of the nineteenth century and are still knitted, sometimes with one thumb and sometimes with two. Two-thumbed mittens were very practical for work because they could be turned around if one thumb became wet or worn out.

Sigríður Halldórsdóttir also notes that the newer mittens are knitted with heavier yarns than previously. To maintain the correct proportions, the patterns have been simplified. Now one stitch is used for a square in a pattern where there used to be four (two by two).

KNITTED SOLES

Inlaid soles with eight-pointed-star patterns are called *rósaleppar.* Other names for the soles are *barðar, illepar,* and *leppar.* These were knitted in garter stitch on two needles with star patterns in several colors covering the whole sole. Children who were learning to knit began with striped soles in garter stitch. The soles can also be knitted in the round by doing two at the same time and cutting them apart afterward. Circular knitted soles are fulled and reinforced with an edging and an extra cloth undersole sewn on. *Slyngdir leppar* is the name of a special Icelandic technique in which bands are woven and sewn directly onto the sole at the same time.

The soles and knitted stockings were worn together inside soft shoes sewn of ox, sheep-, seal-, or fish skin. It used to be that the length of a journey could be measured by how many pairs of shoes were worn out. Seven or more pairs might be needed for a trip across the fells between one farm and another. These soft shoes were worn daily by both men and women well into the twentieth century. Now they are usually worn only with traditional costumes.

WOMEN'S KNITTED JACKETS AND CAPS

The knitted jacket, or *peysuföt,* is a simple, everyday form of Iceland's traditional dress worn by women. It got its name from *peysa,* a dark blue (and later, black), stockinette-knitted wool cardigan. The most unusual feature of these sweaters is the fitting. They are knitted seamlessly to follow the shape of a woman's body. The back piece is finished with a short flap. The body has raglan shaping at the shoulders and sharp decreases toward the waist. A combination of increases and decreases forms the shaping for the breast and elbows. The form is so well defined that these sweaters do not lie flat when stretched out on a board. A small blue or black knitted cap with a long silk tassel called a *skotthúfa* is worn with the outfit. Now, both the *peysa* and the *skotthúfa* are usually sewn from fabric.

LACE KNITTING

Lace knitting came to Iceland sometime toward the end of the nineteenth century via foreign women's magazines, pattern books, and handwork courses. For the most part, lace knitting was used for women's triangular shawls, mittens, and wrist warmers. Both men and women wore wrist warmers which were sometimes knitted with beads threaded onto the yarn and worked in patterns stylish at the time. Shawls were worn with the ends crossed over the chest and tied behind the back. Most shawls were coarse, everyday textiles knitted in garter stitch with two- or three-ply yarns and occasionally decorated with stripes in a contrasting color. Now shawls are spiderweb-thin, triangular or rectangular, and lace-knitted in either a single color or several shades of a color. Shawls knitted in yarn spun only from wool from the sheep's long and lustrous outer coat are certainly magnificent. Lace-knitted shawls are both everyday and holiday apparel.

LOPI

Icelandic sheep are usually shorn in February so that the wool won't felt so much and will be loose and easily processed in today's modern wool factory machinery. Previously, wool was not shorn—it was plucked off in June. The outer coat is called *tog* and the undercoat, *el.* It is easy to tell the difference between the two coats in spring fleeces, but the wool is more blended in winter fleeces, and it is difficult to tell them apart. This doesn't really matter if you are going to handspin the wool. Lopi, a soft, unspun, and untwisted yarn, contains both *tog* and *el,* which makes the yarn stable.

The pattern for this lopi sweater comes from the Alafoss Wool Spinnery. The style is not old, but it has become a classic. It is easy to knit quickly in thick, soft yarns. It took only a few evenings to knit the pictured sweater. Instructions, page 92. Photo: Susanne Pagoldh.

Earlier, "lopi" was the word for carded or combed wool which was drawn out into a thick strand for spinning on a spindle or wheel. When the first wool spinning mills came to Iceland, some of the farmers left fleece which would be carded and drawn out as lopi, ready for spinning. During the 1920s, Elin Guðmundsdóttir Snaehólm tried to knit lopi without spinning it first. Working on a small handknitting machine, she managed to knit a scarf for her husband. She wrote about her experiment in a booklet on handwork in 1923 and the method became popular. It wasn't until the 1930s, though, when knitting became a popular hobby for women, that lopi was used much for handknitting.

One way to make lopi yarn stronger is to skein two or three strands together. Skeining the strands together twists them lightly around each other. Another way is to knit one strand of lopi with a strand of spun yarn. The yarns which are currently sold as lopi are slightly twisted and ready for knitting.

ICELANDIC SWEATERS

Until the Second World War, it was fashionable use lopi to knit lice-pattern sweaters, similar to the Norwegian patterns. The sweaters had broad pattern bands from the shoulders down to the sleeves. The first Icelandic sweaters with patterns around the shoulders like large collars appeared at the end of the 1950s. Elsa Guðjónsson mentions that she saw just such a sweater in 1956 in an issue of a Swedish knitting book published by ICA. The sweater had a circular knitted pattern in red, blue, and white over the shoulders and was called an Icelandic sweater.

She thought that the sweater looked nice and published the pattern in 1957 in *Húsfreyjan,* the Icelandic Women's Union newsletter. Elsa Guðjónsson considers Anna-Lisa Mannheimer Lunn's sweater model, presented to Bohus Knitting in 1947, to be the first circular knitted yoke pattern. Similar patterns also appeared in German and Danish magazines and were sometimes called Greenland designs. They do show similarities to the Greenland beaded collars in pattern and placement (see page 35).

Lopapeysus, lopi sweaters with circular knitted yoke patterns, are still knitted, usually in natural sheep colors, although other colors may also be used. Patterns are usually new but based on traditional Icelandic models.

Gerður Hjörleifsdóttir, director of the Icelandic Handicraft Union, has more than a hundred knitters (both men and women) who produce sweaters for sale. Most of them are older people and parents of small children, who knit at home. Once again, knitting is the source of extra income. The work is not well paid, but the income is tax-free.

Patterns suitable for knitting are found in a hand-illustrated pattern book from 1776. The book is in the National Museum in Reykjavik. Graphed by Elsa E. Guðjónsson.

Traditional patterns for soles. Here every square is a stitch and two rows in garter stitch. At left—jurtapottur, or flowerpot, graphed from a sole in Iceland's National Museum. At right—a stundaglas, hourglass, graphed by Sigriður Halldórsdottír.

NORWAY

ITS SCENERY IS magnificent and sheep are numerous. In the damp sea air, a knitted sweater keeps you warm. Norway isn't just ski slopes! Its long coastline stretches from the North Sea in the south to the Barents Sea in the north. Dramatically beautiful, it is steep and dangerous in many places. Fishing boats and oil platforms dot its seas.

High fells, deep dales, and fjords have all helped to preserve its local character. There are numerous striking folk costumes. When Norwegian immigrants came to the United States from remote highland villages, their clothes, which sported shiny metal clasps and lively motifs, seemed as exotic as those of the American Indians.

There has been great interest in the old folk costumes: since 1947 a state institution, *Bunad*

og folkedraktrådet, has handled questions on copying or adapting folk dress. In certain areas, many old folk costumes are still worn and are sometimes complemented with a knitted garment. One could also say that today's pattern-knitted sweaters are on the way to becoming a new Norwegian folk tradition. Traditional designs pop up in newer styles and in yarn factories' instruction booklets.

Beloved children have many pet names: *strikke, binde, knytte, spitte, spide,* and *spyta* are all words which have been used for knitting. But *knytte* and *binde* also have other meanings, which is a problem for researchers trying to determine how old knitting is. Anne Kjellberg of the Norwegian Folk Museum found notes about old, worn Faroese knitted stockings (*ij gamble wdsledenn bundne ferriiske hosser*) worth four skillings in a

A Fana cardigan knitted in the round and cut. The yarn is heavier than that used in older examples. Instructions (from Rauma) are on page 98. Photo: Susanne Pagoldh.

The older a lusekofta *is, the simpler the embroidery around the neck opening. Detail from a sweater from Valle in Setesdal; now in the Norwegian Folk Museum collection. Photo: Norwegian Folk Museum.*

deceased man's inventory in the accounts for Bergen County from 1566 to 1567. A stockinette-knitted wool fragment was found in an earth layer in a grave opened in Bergen. The fragment is considered to date from just before the Reformation, about 1500.

The Hanseatic city of Bergen in Hordaland was for a long time one of Scandinavia's foremost cities and a center for importation of luxury goods, such as knitted and embroidered silk sweaters (see the photo on page 11). Simpler, everyday clothing was traded, too. Wool sweaters, sweater sleeves, caps, and stockings came from many places in Europe.

"Dirt Poor" was the appellation given to one knitter in Bergen in 1714. In Stavanger in Rogaland, farther south down the coast, two women were accused of being trolls and thieves in 1634. Notes from the trial assert that one woman was in the service of the other: in exchange for room and board she did chores including knitting stockings for her employer.

The body of this star-patterned wool sweater was knitted in one piece, starting at the bottom, up over the shoulders, and back down again. It has no shoulder seams but was sewn at the sides. The armholes were cut open, as was the neck opening, which is edged with velvet. The gauge is about 35 stitches per 10 cm (4 in). The sweater is from Sunnhordaland and is now in the Historical Museum in Bergen. Photo: Ann-Mari Olsen / Historical Museum, The University in Bergen.

If one believes the statutes for the Home for Women and Servants in Trondhjem and the Widow's Home in Bergen, people were already knitting by the middle of the seventeenth century. It should be noted that knitting was most closely associated with society's lowest levels: thieves and the poor.

Eventually, a school was established in Bergen where children could learn to knit. Later, it was fashionable for girls to knit, which saved many riksdalers, as otherwise, everyday sweaters had be be bought from England.

STARS

The eight-pointed star which shines forth from so many Norwegian sweaters and mittens is found in many cultures and is one of our most common textile motifs. The eight-petaled rose, as it is called in Norway, was found in knitted form even in thirteenth-century Spain. A museum in Burgos has a star-patterned knitted silk pillow cover which may have been knitted by Arabs. The same star design decorated the upper class's silk sweaters during the 1600s and appeared later on peasant women's tight-fitting wool sweaters. The star is also common in the Norwegian picture-weaving tradition and on *rosetepper,* woven bed covers from Vestland.

Fjellrosen is the name of several variants of a pattern with eight-pointed stars and diagonal boxes. The pattern, which goes back to the 1840s, was knitted on men's Sunday and church-wear sweaters in Fjell on the island of Sotra outside Bergen. Often, the sweaters were knitted in dark indigo blue and white yarn, with the date and initials knitted at the bottom of a white knitted welt 20 to 30 cm (8 to 12 in) long. The white section couldn't be seen when the sweater was tucked into trousers. A shirt was worn under the sweater and a vest over it. Sometimes, a sweater sewn of wadmal, or felted fabric, was worn over the vest as protection against the North Sea's winds. Those who had the means had one sweater just for Sunday non-church wear, another only for wearing to church, and a third if necessary for every day. After being worn, the church sweater was aired out in the sun so it would be ready for the next Sunday.

CARDIGANS FROM FANA

Fana, which is just south of Bergen, gave its name to Fana sweaters (*Fanatrøjen*), one of the most popular knitted garments in Norway (see page 43). The sweater, or cardigan, was originally part of the traditional man's costume in Fana and evolved from an everyday undersweater which

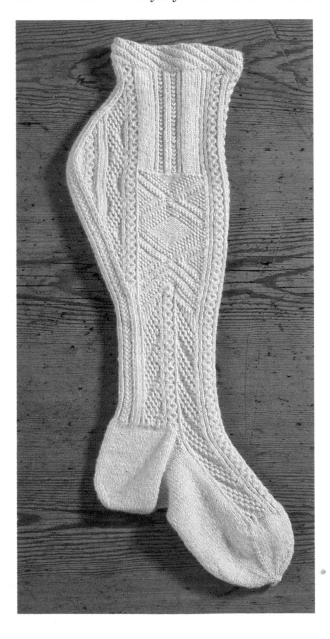

was worn under the vest and tucked into the trousers. This sweater was narrow and tight-fitting and had slits at the neck and cuffs which could be buttoned like the cuffs on shirt sleeves. Old photographs show that the sweater was worn about 1870.

It is believed that the Fana sweater became a cardigan with a front opening and buttons about 1900. Sometimes, the buttons were old coins inherited from the time of Christian IV (1588–1648). The yarn, a fine two-ply in natural black or brown and white, was knitted in the round on fine double-pointed 1.5 mm (US 000) needles. Normally, the hip-length sweaters had drop shoulders that looked broad and slid down on the arms so that the sleeves could be knitted shorter. The front opening was cut and edged with woven bands. A favorite band had red hearts on a white background. The neck opening was squared and lined with cotton cloth.

The style and cut, especially that of the neckline, of Fana cardigans have changed in modern times, beginning at the time of Norway's independence (1905). The Fana sweater has certainly been popular for skiwear. Children's sweaters were often knitted in red and white or blue and white. When the Germans occupied Norway during the Second World War, the sweater became a national symbol for solidarity in the areas around Bergen.

LICE-PATTERNED CARDIGANS

Men's sweaters from Valle in Setesdal (a long valley in southern Norway) have also found a secure place in the folk costume tradition. In Sweden, the sweaters are better known as Norwegian *lusekofta*—lice-patterned cardigans. The white-dotted sweaters have been known since the 1840s, and many old ones have been preserved with folk costumes in Setesdal.

The sweaters had white patterns on a black background, white lower edges, and drop shoulders. The neck openings and sleeves were edged with black embroidered fabric and decorative buttons. The neck opening was fastened with a clasp of tin or silver. Older sweaters often had

To save black yarn, the lower edges of Setesdal sweaters were knitted with white. The ribbed welt was invisible when tucked into trousers. Merete Lütken, who knitted the sweater in the picture, used the white welt as decoration. The sweater also has very simple embroidery around the neck opening as was traditional but features modern ribbed cuffs on the sleeves. This sweater is a good example of how an old garment can be adapted for modern tastes. Instructions: page 85. A slipover sweater from the 1950s has been cut open as a cardigan. The front edges have been strengthened with decorative bands, and the cuffs are buttoned and embroidered. Photo: Susanne Pagoldh.

(left) A krotasåkka from Bygland in Setesdal. Both men's and women's stockings were knitted with white yarn. Women's stockings were dyed black afterward. This stocking was knitted by Olav Aamlid from an older model that is now in the Norwegian Folk Museum collection. Photo: Norwegian Folk Museum.

side seams and sleeve gussets, details carried over from fabric shirts. Threads for embroidery were factory-made four-ply wool yarns that were soft and loosely spun. Red was the most common color, but green, blue, yellow, lilac, rose, brown, and white were also used. Older sweaters had very simple embellishments while newer ones are more colorful and gaudy.

Traditionally, the men wore the sweaters tucked into black wadmal trousers with suspenders. Like carpenter's pants, these trousers reached high up on the chest and had goatskin pieces to reinforce the seat. A short vest with heavy silver jewelry was worn on top. *Krotasokkar*, white wool stockings with compli-

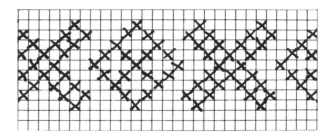

(left) Kross og kringle *(cross and circle, or X's and O's) is a pattern often found on Setesdal* lusekoftor.

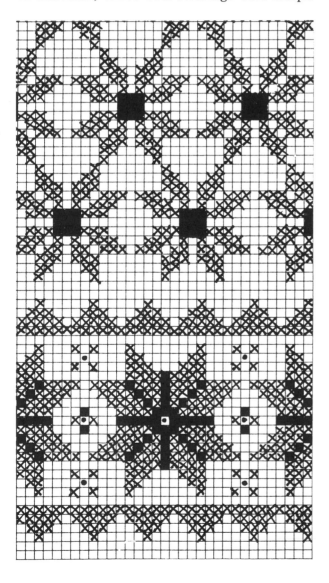

A luskufte *from Valle in Setesdal, knitted in hand-spun wool yarn, edged with black cloth and embroidered with wool yarn. The sweater is in the Norwegian Folk Museum, Oslo. Photo: Norwegian Folk Museum.*

(far left) Body and cuff patterns drawn from a wool sweater from Sunnhordaland. Color photo, page 45.

(left) This triangular shawl, which is almost boomerang shaped, has ends that are just over 1.5 meters long (1⅝ yd) so that they cross the chest, go around the body and then back to the front to be tied in a knot at the waist. The Norwegian Folk Museum has a similar black wool shawl from Dale in Sunnefjord dated from the end of the nineteenth century. It has a lace border at the lower edge, and the rest of it is knitted in garter stitch. Instructions for the shawl pictured here come from Norwegian Handicrafts and are on page 108. Photo: Susanne Pagoldh.

catcd twisted patterns, were worn on the feet. Women also wore these stockings, but theirs were black.

It has been said that an enterprising woman, Gyro Rygnestad, was the first to sell a Setesdal sweater to someone outside the area. In 1938, she told Anna Grostol, a Norwegian needlework teacher who traveled around and collected information on handicrafts, that she sold the first woman's sweater in 1934 to a wholesaler in Kristiansand. The year after that, she knit a sweater without any embroidery—a man's Setesdal sweater in a sports model. At first, the people in Valle thought that it looked cheap, but the sweater sold well and the fashion caught on. It wasn't too long before the sweaters were machine knitted and some were cut open for cardigans. Most were knitted in black and white, but they could be made in other colors if the customer wanted. Many of these sweaters ended up in the United States.

A new fashion wave hit during the 1960s, and the cardigans were edged with embroidery along the whole front and buttoned with shiny clasps. The sweaters became acceptable formal wear and could be worn instead of a jacket.

Today's *lusekoftor* which are made for sale are knitted in heavier yarns than those for the knitter or her own family. Some unbelievably well-knitted sweaters are still made, and even boys will take up their needles when they want something exceptional.

MARIUS GANSEYS

In 1953, the designer Unn Sóiland Dale used the old patterns from Setesdal, particularly *kross og kringle* (cross and circle, or X's and O's) as the starting point for a sweater that became one of Norwegian knitting's biggest sellers: the Marius gansey. The word *genser,* or in Swedish *gensare,* comes from English and means a wool sweater. *Gens* comes from Guernsey, an island in the English Channel where marine blue fishermen's

sweaters have been knitted for quite a long time. The first Marius ganseys featured the Norwegian flag colors: a blue bottom with patterns in red and white over the chest and shoulders.

The ethnologist Gerd Aarsland Rosander has researched the history behind the sweater and how it came to have the name Marius. At the beginning of the 1950s, two slalom skiers, the brothers Stein and Marius Eriksen, were popular idols, like today's Ingemar Stenmark and Björn Borg in Sweden. They exemplified Norwegian-

The instructions for this Setesdal-patterned sweater are from Rauma. A red cap complements this outfit which has all the colors of the Norwegian flag. Instructions for the sweater are on page 93; those for the hat are on page 114. Photo: Susanne Pagoldh.

ness and youth. Because Stein participated in the 1952 Olympics and no one wanted to risk his amateur status, the sweater was named after Marius, who was also a slalom star. A yarn manufacturer published the knitting instructions with a portrait of Marius Eriksen on the front.

In only the past five years, more than 100,000 copies of the knitting instructions for Marius ganseys have been printed and sold, according to Gerd Rosander. Instructions for the Fana sweater have sold equally well during that period. But when one thinks of how many instructions are borrowed and sweaters copied from those already knitted, the figures are much higher and competitive with machine-made models. It just goes to show that knitting is an important economic activity in Norway.

PROTEST CAPS

"Warning. Red caps. The wearing of red caps has lately become so prevalent that they are now considered a type of protest. Wearing of these caps is forbidden beginning on Thursday, 26 February 1942. From that day forward, the caps will be confiscated from whoever is wearing one. . . ." This was a public announcement from the police in Trondhjem. Wearing a red cap was considered a political statement against the Germans. It was such a strong symbol that elves' red caps on Christmas cards were censored that winter.

Caps as a political symbol were nothing new—pointed caps had been a symbol of protest long before and during the French Revolution in 1789. In Norway, the red cap has a very long tradition. People preferred to buy them ready-made, and in certain areas, homemade caps were thought to be unusual. In 1782, the Enighed Factory started up in Stor-Elvdal. Their machine-made caps became highly sought after. Miners working in the Roros, Norway, copper mines were enchanted with them because they had to be bought in Norway and thus symbolized a business trip. At home in Sweden, the caps were a sign that the wearer had traveled far away.

In Norway, it is said that "caps follow the owner to the grave." Men slept with a cap on the

head but were otherwise stark naked. Caps came off only in church on Sundays. Caps could also be worn under hats. In Hordaland, in the archipelago outside Bergen, the men wore dark blue caps with colorful patterns, usually of stars. The caps' lower edges were embroidered with checks in red, yellow, and white. All of the cap's colors were used in the tassel. In Rogaland, similar caps were knitted; they were very long and heavily patterned, and edged with pile.

WRAPAROUND SHAWLS

"Men wear caps and women wear shawls." Shawls could be knitted or crocheted and were triangular with long points or bands. The ends were wrapped in a cross over the chest, backward around the back, then around to the front again, giving the old shawls and their wearers a pretty silhouette. The widest section hung over the shoulders like angel wings, and the tied bands

made the wearer look slim. Large shawls were also warm enough for sleeping in under a skin rug.

SWEATERS FOR TOURISTS

Wool sweaters with patterns that resemble a circular knitted collar over the shoulders are very popular presents to take home from a trip to Norway. These colorful sweaters light up many souvenir shops in airports and large hotels. The strong colors are as closely associated with Norway as the natural sheep colors are with Iceland. It is difficult to say how this came to be—in the Faroe Islands they are called Greenland patterns.

During the period between the two world wars, sweaters were knitted in the round in Norway. Gerd Rosander remembers from her childhood in the 1930s and 1940s that many knitters worked the patterned yoke in the round, but with the difference that decreases were made in four particular places. The result was a sweater with distinctive raglan shaping. The Greenland beaded collars (see page 35) could have been the source for the new way of knitting with the decreases evenly spaced over a round (see page 40). But circular needles are certainly older than that. We can trace them at least back to the fashion magazine *Dagmar* from 1881.

Lice, stars, and reindeer also decorate the offerings in the gift shops. The hangtags promise that they are handknitted in 100 percent Norwegian wool, but the odd statement "Made in Sri Lanka" often follows. The Norwegian yarn company Dale has hired knitters in Sri Lanka to meet the huge demand for Norwegian garments.

SELBU

The famous Norwegian moose and reindeer designs originated in Selbu knitting. The familiar star patterns or *sjenn-rosa* and other figurative designs are named after natural objects or the area where they were first made.

Selbu lies in Sør-Trøndelag at the same latitude as Jämtland. Businesses still cross the bor-

ders as they did in earlier times, and perhaps the knitting patterns were spread in this way. Even on the Swedish side, one finds graphic black-and-white or brown-and-white patterns.

Previously, Selbu had been best known for its millstones. When millstone sales ceased at the turn of the century, knitting came into prominence. After the First World War, knitting was so strong that it gained real economic importance. A

The Selbu-patterned sweater can also be cut open for a cardigan and edged with bands in the traditional way. Instructions from Rauma are on page 94. Photo: Susanne Pagoldh.

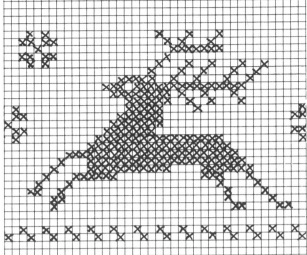

The mitten (instructions, page 109) is knitted from a pair of Selbu mittens in the Norwegian Folk Museum collection. Instructions for the glove are from Rauma and are on page 111. Photo: Susanne Pagoldh.

The reindeer (far right) is part of a Rauma pattern.

The stocking to the left is dated 1870 and is in the Norwegian Folk Museum. The one to the right is knitted following instructions from Rauma on page 117. Photo: Norwegian Folk Museum, Susanne Pagoldh.

handicraft center was started in the 1930s. The center procured yarn, standardized patterns, and bought and sold garments. Another responsibility was to control and preserve the well-known Selbu quality. Garments were graded into various classes, and quality was guaranteed.

Usually, it was the women who knitted, but during times of crisis and job shortages, the needles even clicked in the hands of men and boys. Although the work has never been well paid, it was the means of survival for many families.

According to family tradition, it was Marit Emstad (born in 1841) who knitted the first pair of Selbu mittens sometime during the 1850s. The mittens are said to have had black stars on a white background. Pattern knitting spread in the village, and it wasn't long before the girls in Selbu knitted patterns with all sorts of figures and flourishes. Marit continued knitting throughout her life. She adapted patterns from other crafts such as weaving or woodcarving. She also invented new patterns from recognizable forms in nature and her home.

Another energetic woman was Beret Aune (born in 1856). When she was young and newly married, she went with her children and husband to America, where he had found work in a brick factory. As a way of funding a school for the children, Beret gathered the women in the area and taught them how to knit mittens. She then

Patterns drawn from a Lapland mitten from Kautokeino. The wool mittens, which are in the Norwegian Folk Museum in Oslo, are knitted in dark violet, sky blue, green, red, and white.

wedding guests expected to take home mittens, but the bride didn't have to knit all of them—the women guests helped.

A few days before the wedding, the women guests would show up with mittens for the bride. The mittens were hung up in a particular order in the bride's loft. For large weddings, there could be a hundred or so pairs of mittens. It was the bride's duty to see that each pair of the mittens went to the right man. A woman who had knitted a pair of mittens got to take them home again with her husband. It was exciting for the young and unmarried women to see who got their mittens.

Nowadays, it is usually older women in Selbu who knit for sale. The yarn used is thicker than that used formerly for presents. Clear colors like red or blue on a white background are preferred for mittens. The patterns have become so widespread and well known that now almost all two-color patterns in Norway are referred to as Selbu, no matter where the pattern originated.

ON THE HANDS AND FEET

Embroidered mittens, half mittens, and gauntlets were all clerical apparel. Half mittens freed the fingers for turning pages in the psalm book. They also kept the palms warm in the cold, unheated churches. Half mittens were also practical for women who knitted while they walked. Both men and women wore *pulsvantar* (wrist warmers), some of which were elegantly knitted with threaded beads (see also page 34). They were warm and also decorously hid worn-out or dirty sleeves.

Otherwise, most people wore coarse socks or work mittens. These were usually made with undyed yarn because they wore out so soon. Several pairs might be needed for one season. Work mittens could also be made in two-end knitting for extra strength.

To make socks stronger, goat hair was blended with wool. Black wool and white goat hair made a salt-and-pepper yarn. Occasionally, the socks were knitted with an open heel, that is, a hole instead of a heel. This was done so that

went around the neighborhood selling them. After the school was built, they knitted for a church. Eventually, Beret moved back to Selbu and started up a new women's union—a bridge was needed, and they built it!

WEDDING GIFTS IN SELBU

A wedding in Selbu involved a great deal of work. A girl who was to marry needed plenty of time to knit. First and foremost, a beautiful pair of stockings had to be knitted for the groom. The groom's father, brothers, and in-laws also expected pattern-knitted stockings. The bride gave cloth to the groom's mother, sisters, and sisters-in-law. One way to obtain the cloth was to exchange knitting for it at the shop. All of the male they could be drawn on over shoes or other socks like an extra shoe as protection against the snow. The stocking feet could also be reinforced by a wadmal sole. In Nordmore, these large, heavy, ribbed socks are called *raggå*. In Oppland, cow hair was blended in the yarn for outer stockings or *utapåhoser* that had long legs and were held on the feet with straps. *Tålabber* were a shorter style of these stockings.

Blending in hair from animals or humans is a well-known method for strengthening yarn. Hair can be blended in during spinning or held together with the wool yarn while knitting. In that way, more hair can be added at the points where strength is most needed. Human hair was often mixed with wool for mittens and stockings to be worn by sailors and mine workers.

Fishermen wore mittens with two thumbs. In certain districts, these were called *sjøvotter* or *hvalfangervotter*. The thumb that wasn't being used was stuffed into the mitten so that it wouldn't be in the way. The mittens were knitted extra large and then well fulled in warm soapy water or, on the More coast, in fish broth. Gallbladders from codfish were stuffed inside mittens when they were washed. The mittens were then pressed hard so that the gallbladders burst and their contents—natural cleansers—permeated the wool.

MITTENS FROM FINNMARK

The Laplanders' homelands stretch from Røros in the south, north and eastward to Kolahalv Island in the Soviet Union. Their languages and clothing vary from area to area, particularly between the coast and inland, but all are related.

Traditionally the Laplanders wore fur mittens in the winter. Both mittens and shoes were stuffed with warm, soft hay. After the nomadic Laplanders encountered trading shops and knitting, they replaced the hay inside their fur mittens with knitted mittens. In time, many Laplanders settled in one place and raised sheep.

In Kautokeino in Finnmark, in northern Lapland, mittens (*faccâk*, in Lapp) have been knitted

since the end of the nineteenth century. The mittens are patterned in red, blue, and green on a white background. No pair is exactly like another. In the Norwegian Folk Museum in Oslo, there are several pairs that have patterns over the entire outer side but only halfway up on the palm side. The mittens have two-end knitting patterns on the lower edge, and some also have tassels.

In Sør-Varanger in Finnmark, on the border with the Soviet Union, white wool mittens are knitted with red, blue, and white patterns around the upper wrist. The patterns are adapted from woven bands and the familiar eight-pointed star. Nelly Must in Jarfjord has collected and written down the old patterns. The results of her work have now been collected in the Sør-Varanger Museum in Kirkenes.

Nelly Must knitted this wool man's mitten in a pattern from the Varanger district in Finnmark. The mitten is in the Sør-Varanger Museum in Kirkenes. Instructions, page 113. Photo: Susanne Pagoldh

SWEDEN

THE FOPPISH KING ERIK XIV is reputed to be the first person in Scandinavia to have worn knitted silk stockings. The stockings were imported in 1562, just one year after England's Queen Elizabeth I got her first pair. Knitted stockings, which elegantly showed off the wearer's legs, were high fashion on the continent during that time, particularly for men who wore short trousers. We can't be sure what Erik's stockings looked like, but they must have been splendid considering the price, which was equivalent to the annual wages of a chamber valet.

During the 1600s knitted silk sweaters were imported for those who could afford them. They were true luxury garments, decorated with gold or silver threads. Several of these sweaters have been preserved in Norway (see page 11), and Sweden has two of them. Star and flower motifs, similar to those on the silk sweaters, were later knitted on sweaters and sleeves in simpler mate-rials for farmers and shopkeepers well into the nineteenth century. Several eighteenth-century women's sweaters from Halland have been pre-served. They are knitted in wool, cotton, or linen, but take their inspiration from the seventeenth-century styles.

BINGE—KNITTING IN HALLAND

The art of knitting (*sticka, binda, binga*) was known early in Halland, which was a part of Denmark until 1645. The area was poor, the earth sandy and unfruitful, and there were few possi-bilities for earning an income. In the southern parts of the province, stocking and sweater knit-ting was a much needed source of support. At certain times, knitting was rewarded well enough that farming was neglected, and it was difficult to find servants. Halland's sheep couldn't provide all the wool that was needed, and so wool was imported from Denmark and Iceland.

The Nordic Museum has a sweater from Ullared in Halland with the initials O I P S and the date 1898 knitted in a rectangle on the chest. This detail has been kept for the updated version of the sweater, which has a ribbed neck opening and contrasting patterns on the side seams and sleeves. The old Ullared sweaters often had crocheted edgings on the neck and sleeves. Similar sweaters have also been knitted in the Varberg district. Instructions, page 88. Photo: Susanne Pagoldh.

Magna Brita Cracau, a Dutch woman from the Vallens estate in Våxtorp, is known for having spread the art of knitting in Halland. According to Dean Pehr Osbeck, either Magna or her Dutch servants taught knitting to the people on the estate sometime during the 1650s. The tenants could pay their taxes with knitting. The technique quickly spread from Vallens into Våxtorp, and traditions were begun which are still carried on. The knitters from Våxtorp became known for their skills in knitting patterns with several colors.

More commonly, they knitted simple undyed garments like undersweaters and stockings, but pattern-knitted sweaters with several colors (*plättabing*) were also knitted, as well as single-color relief-patterned sweaters (*fläckabing*) that had star designs worked in purl stitches on a stockinette ground. Knitters in the districts of Laholm, Halmstad, Hasslöv, Hök, and Tönnersjö were specialists at knitting wool stockings quickly. The stitches were large and loose but became firm when fulled in soapy water. The army was furnished with several thousand pairs of stockings. Whole regiments of soldiers marched to war with Halland stockings on their feet.

During the autumn, the poor people of Halland would go to the richer area of Skåne, searching for work. In exchange for room and board or cash, they did spinning and knitting on farmsteads. Supposedly, some of them wandered to the Danish island of Amager in Öresund. Knitting was looked down on there—it was something lowly that Swedes did!

Peddlers travelled from farm to farm in the Skåne area, selling knitted garments. They would buy wool from one farm and leave it for spinning and knitting at another where there were more workers. The finished goods could be carried on a journey that stretched over a huge area of the country.

FISHERMEN'S SWEATERS

During the nineteenth century, the traveling peddlers were put out of business. Sweater merchants from Laholm and Göteborg began distrib-

uting wool for knitting sweaters and stockings. A certain amount of wool, usually barely enough, was reckoned on for a particular number of garments. The wool had to be carded, spun, and sometimes dyed. This wasn't just a small business concern—during one year in the 1850s, 96,000 sweaters, 66,000 pairs of whole and half stockings, and 28,000 pairs of mittens were knitted in the Laholm district alone! Even though these mass-produced garments were thick and loosely knitted, their quality was fairly high; the patterns used in knitting them were intricate,

Krok, a pattern from the Knitting Cooperative's archives. When it was drawn in 1912, it was regarded as an old pattern. It is similar to patterns knitted on the Shetland Islands. Photo: Susanne Pagoldh.

This pheasant design is one of the older ones in the Knitting Cooperative's collection in Halmstad. Photo: Susanne Pagoldh.

Bjärbo is one of the oldest and most popular designs of the Knitting Cooperative. It is thought to have been knitted in Halland since the eighteenth century.

and the short floats on the inside of the garment gave the fabric substance.

Women knitted the bodies of the large fishermen's sweaters, and men and children knitted the sleeves. Two people could sit opposite one another and knit on the same sweater body. One classic sweater pattern is called *jyske* because the pattern was thought to have come to Halland from Jutland. The Nordic Museum in Stockholm has an old Halland fisherman's sweater with the *jyske* design knitted in light purple on a natural white ground. *Skák og teinur* (slants and sticks), a similar pattern from the Faroe Islands (see page 24), has also been knitted in that colorway. Another typical Halland sweater pattern has red stripes and blue checks on a white ribbed background.

KNITTING COOPERATIVE

By the end of the nineteenth century, the knitters in Halland were having difficulty selling their work. The West Götaland shops failed, and handknitting ceased to be so highly paid when it had to compete with machine-made garments. In 1907, Berta Borgström, a doctor's wife from Laholm, founded the Knitting Cooperative to help the jobless people in the area and to put new life into old knitting traditions. She recruited her first handknitters from the farms around Vallen in Våxtorp. She imported soft fine-wool yarns from England, and the knitting was soon under way.

For the first few years, mostly military socks and sweaters and hunting mittens were made. Knee-length pattern-knitted sports cardigans with striped edgings and ribbing sold well. The department store MEA, Militär Ekiperings AB, and the royal household in Stockholm were among the first customers. Crown Princess Margareta and Princess Maria ordered caps and jackets for the members of their golf club. Princes Gustaf Adolf and Sigvard were photographed bobsledding in *bjärbo*-patterned sports sweaters from the Knitting Cooperative.

Beata and Lars Petter Jönsson were also good advertising during those patriotic times.

They wore traditional Halland costumes and worked together knitting sweater bodies for exhibitions and advertisements. During many of the cooperative's first summers, its members sat under parasols and sold knitting at fashionable sea resorts like Båstad, Marstrand, and Strömstad.

After the cooperative started, traditional patterns from the district were quickly collected. Its most popular pattern throughout the years has been *bjärbo*, which is said to have been knitted in Halland since the eighteenth century. The Hishult woman's costume has a *bjärbo*-patterned waist-length sweater knitted in red and black and cut open at the front. Nowadays, *bjärbo* is usually knitted in red and blue on a white ground. Pattern-knitted fiddler's caps and long, patterned double caps were traditional men's garments in Halland collected by the Knitting Cooperative.

KNITTING TODAY

During its first years, the cooperative employed about a hundred knitters. Today, only

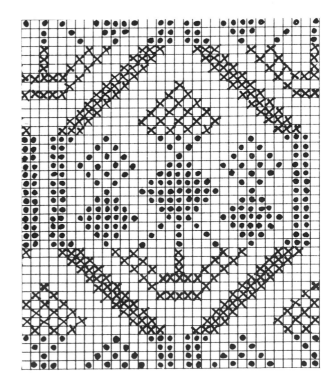

A man's sweater from Kungshamn in Bohus province was the model for this updated sweater. The old sweater, which is in the Nordic Museum, has a knitted side stripe, triangular neck and underarm gussets (see page 8), striped ribbing that is slit at the sides, and the initials A K S knitted in the lower edge. Here the sleeve stitches were picked up around the armhole and knitted down to the cuffs. On the old sweater, the sleeves were sewn in. The simple overall pattern is not limited to Bohus province—it was also knitted in Norway, Latvia, and on the Faroe Islands. Instructions, page 89. Photo: Susanne Pagoldh.

A woman's wool circular-knitted sweater from Vemmenhög district in southern Skåne. The neck opening is lined with linen cloth and edged with a narrow velvet band and a silk band 5 cm (2 in) wide. It is part of the Nordic Museum's collections. Photo: Birgit Brånvall/Nordic Museum.

about ten knitters work for what has been renamed the Halland Knitting Cooperative. One of them is Inga-Britt Dahlin of Laholm, who knits only by special order. The customer chooses the patterns, colors, and style. Inga-Britt has been knitting since she was five years old, when her mother taught her how. At first, she knitted only for her own family, but later she became a professional knitter.

When Inga-Britt has an order for a cloak or jacket, both popular garments now, she knits both the body and sleeves on circular needles. Both sleeves are knitted at once in a long tube. When all the pieces have been knitted, she gives them to her good friend Barbro Nilsson for assembly. The assembly (called *brättningen*) is unique to Halland knitting: the knitted fabric is cut and handled just like woven cloth. It's been done this way since the cooperative was started.

Many who knit have someone else do the assembly because they are afraid to cut the fabric, but Barbro Nilsson is a trained seamstress and isn't the least hesitant to set her scissors into the stitches. She has been assembling garments for the cooperative for 20 years, and she knows that knitting doesn't rip out so easily. Proper *binge* should be so tightly knitted that a finished garment can be hung on a coat hanger without stretching. That means it's knitted well enough that it can be cut up also.

Barbro cuts the circular knitted tubes open, presses them out flat, and cuts out the pattern parts. She pin-bastes the pieces on the person who will get the garment and cuts and shapes the darts, pockets, and collar. She cuts out the armholes when the basted pieces are being tried on. Then she sews the garment together on a machine using a tricot stitch.

The old patterns which were collected at the beginning of this century are still in use, although with new color combinations and styles. In the 1940s and 1950s, waist-length jackets were knitted. During the 1960s, longer jackets were in style. Now all sorts of jackets, capes, and outfits are knitted. When the royal couple visited Halland during a royal tour in 1980, Queen Silvia received a knitted poncho constructed by the

handicraft consultant Kersti Nilsson. A strange garment for Sweden, but it had many of the traditional Halland patterns on it.

Interest in the old Halland designs has increased during the 1980s. During the last few years, Inga-Britt Dahlin has conducted several knitting courses. A group of Lebanese women were among her students, but very few men have participated in the courses.

BOHUS KNITTING

Closely patterned sweaters similar to those knitted in Halland have also been knitted in Bohus province. The Nordic Museum has an old man's sweater from Sotenäs which is rich in detail (see page 8). The neck and the sleeves have triangular gussets, making the garment fit well. The welt has side vents and a monogram knitted in. The seams in the body and sleeves are marked with distinctive patterns. These decorative and practical details were adapted from garments sewn of woven cloth. Similar details were also knitted into fishermen's sweaters in England and on the islands of Jersey and Guernsey.

The Bohus Knitting Cooperative, like the Halland Knitting Cooperative, was started in 1939 to help women in need of work. Their work made Bohus knitting famous. Sales of their stylish cardigans and sweaters made with wool and angora yarns were at their height during the 1950s, when the garments were exported to the United States. The cooperative closed down in 1969.

SWEATERS FROM SKÅNE

There is a rich textile tradition in fertile Skåne, but knitting was not considered as prestigious an occupation as, for example, weaving. Knitting was usually done by poor Skåne residents or migrant workers from Halland. Peddlers also came to Skåne with their wares.

Even during the 1700s, people in Skåne wore knitted stockings, *spede* sweaters, and wool undersweaters. Similar sweaters knitted in Denmark were called night sweaters (see page 22).

Spede sweaters got their name from *speda*, which means a knitting needle. *Spede* sweaters were knitted in the round with a thin, tightly twisted wool yarn and were narrow and tight-fitting. They were usually worn under a vest so that only the sleeves were visible. After being knitted, some of these sweaters were fulled so well that individual stitches could not be distinguished.

Spede sweaters were always knitted in one color with relief patterns on the sides of the body and on the sleeves. Occasionally they had allover patterns. One popular pattern was the eight-pointed star. The neck opening and the lower edges of the sleeves were often decorated with silk or velvet bands which were sewn on. In the western parts of Skåne, green sweaters were most often worn during the summer; blue or black sweaters were for winter, and red ones for festivals and holidays.

ON GOTLAND AND ÖLAND

People on Öland and Gotland have been knitting garments to sell since at least the end of the seventeenth century and possibly even longer. Trading on the Baltic was lively during the Middle Ages, and the Hanseatic city of Visby was a

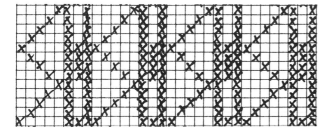

A Gotland gauntlet mitten. Pattern and details were adapted from Hermanna Stengård's collection at Gotland Handicrafts. Instructions, page 113. Photo: Susanne Pagoldh.

Wool stockings from Bollebygd (left) and Skåning district (right) in western Gotland. The patterns on the stocking at the left (see diagram) are reminiscent of the so-called "flame yarn" stripes which occur when cloth is woven with ikat-dyed warp. Here the effect is achieved by using yarn in two shades of blue. The red patterned bands in the stocking on the right are knitted with ikat-dyed yarn. Both stockings are in the Nordic Museum. Photo: Birgit Brånvall / Nordic Museum.

center with trading connections deep into Europe.

The West Götaland peddlers were early traders with Gotland. Knitting (called *sticksöm* on Gotland) was exchanged for linen and other goods. People from Öland traded with Smålanders and got flax, linen, and hemp in exchange for knitting.

During the eighteenth and nineteenth centuries, Gotland sweaters were an important item of trade and were shipped overseas to Stockholm by the so-called "sweater hags", who were actually ambitious businesswomen. The Gotland sweaters traveled from Stockholm northward to Hälsingland and Härjedalen. The account books for the Hudiksvall businessman Per Högberg list three trips to the capital during 1786. He sold weavings, skins, and butter in Stockholm and bought large quantities of Gotland sweaters and wool stockings. He took these items with him to markets in Delsbo, Färila, Jättendal, and Bjuråker, traveling by boat, horse, and wagon.

We don't know for certain what the Gotland sweaters looked like. The coarsest ones had cow hair blended in the yarn and were worn for heavy work. The finest ones were made of lustrous wool, decorated with figures like columbines, hourglasses, and red deer. Other sweaters were described as striped, checked, multicolored, patent-knitted (a way of knitting which gives a ribbed surface or a spongy texture), simple, and one-colored in white wool or in white ribbing with alternating patterns in red and blue.

On Gotland, knitting yarn was spun from

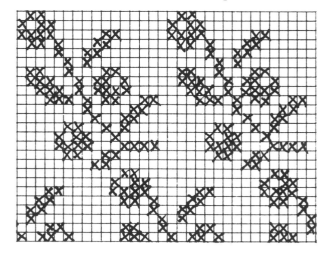

This pattern from Hermanna Stengård's collection is called "lingon sprig".

spring wool. People knitted every day, but the days between Christmas and Epiphany were considered knitting holidays. Traditionally, it was thought that the sheep would not thrive if a spindle or spinning wheel were used during that period. It was also believed that a garment wouldn't come out right if scroll patterns were knitted counterclockwise on it.

One of the old Gotland sagas tells of an old woman who was working outside and longing for her husband. While she was walking along, she knitted a new pair of mittens for him. After she had been walking a while, she met the fearsome giant Hobersgubben, who sat on a rock and was shivering in the cold, gray weather. She felt sorry for him and gave him the mittens which she had just finished. He was so pleased with the warm wool mittens that he gave her three wishes.

Gotland mittens characteristically have all-over patterns which are continued onto the thumb. Some have a curving pattern around the wrist. Besides mittens and sweaters, quite a few stockings, caps, suspenders, belts, and bands were knitted.

Thanks to Hermanna Stengård, an elementary school teacher from Rone parish, many of the old Gotland stocking and mitten patterns have been preserved. She went around to the farms, seeking out and collecting traditional patterns. Her findings were published in the book *Gotland Knitting* in 1925, and her collection is now at Gotland Handicrafts in Visby.

Little of the Öland knitting has survived. Its mittens have patterns similar to those found on Gotland. On north Öland, heavy work mittens with two thumbs were common. Natural-colored handspun wool was used for everyday garments. When machine-spun English wool became available at the beginning of this century, black-and-white and black-and-green combinations became popular.

SWEATER SLEEVES FROM WEST DALARNA

In Dalarna, most garments are knitted in two-end, or twined, knitting. The technique,

tvåändsstickning, has been used for decoration and for knitting patterned edges on sweaters, stockings, socks, and mittens in the Nordic countries since at least the seventeenth century. The technique was especially useful for stocking heels and work mittens which had to withstand hard wear.

One outstanding garment in Dalarna's rich textile tradition is the jacket worn by both men and women in West Dalarna, and particularly in the parishes of Gagnef and Floda. The sweaters, which have been knitted since the early 1800s, have richly patterned sleeves in twined knitting sewn onto a cloth body. The sweaters were worn both inside and outside, on weekdays and Sundays, but never in church. When one of these

sweaters was worn out, it still found service as work clothing. The women's sweaters were waist-length and, beginning in the 1870s (when sewing machines became available), usually had machine embroidery on the chest and on the bands at the lower edges of the sleeves. Men's sweaters were hip-length, single- or double-breasted, and occasionally had pockets.

The sleeves were knitted in the round in natural white and natural black unwashed wool yarn, and dyed after they were knitted—most often red. Then the already dense structure was fulled, and the natural black color took on an even deeper shade. The importance of making sturdy sleeves is shown by the number preserved in Dalarna's museum in Falun.

This type of jacket was part of the folk costumes in Nås, Floda, and Gagnef parishes, and the jackets are still knitted today, although in ordinary pattern knitting. Green wadmal is used for the bodies while the sleeves are knitted with red and black wool yarn. Because two colors are used in the pattern, the threads are twisted on the back side, but the structure looks quite different from that of twined knitting.

Patterns on the sweaters vary from district to district, and there can also be small differences within one parish. The form of the sleeves also varies. The oldest ones were narrow. At the end of the nineteenth century, the very wide leg-of-mutton sleeves were in vogue, but by the twentieth century, the sleeves were again narrow and fitted.

HÄLSINGLAND SWEATERS

Flax production was more widespread in Hälsingland than sheep breeding or wool production; linen was well known for its lovely luster and high quality. The income from linen was lucrative, at least for some farmers.

Both men and women wore showy, pattern-knitted sweaters. In Delsbo and Bjuråker, the sweaters had strong, striking patterns in red, black, and green wool with details in white cotton yarn. In the nineteenth century, the stark white

LOVIKKA MITTENS

Erika Aittamaa knitted the first pair of Lovikka mittens in 1892. When a woodsman wanted some particularly thick and strong mittens, she spun an extra-heavy wool yarn. She knitted two pairs which were so thick that she thought they would last several winters. But the man who ordered them thought that she had ruined the wool. She took the "spoiled" mittens back home and washed them several times and then carded them, first on the inside and then on the outside, to soften them. The result was a new way of finishing mittens. The soft, brushed mittens became popular, and the style quickly spread throughout the district. Erika Aittamaa got a number of orders for the mittens, which she began to decorate with turned-back cuffs embroidered with multicolored wool threads.

More and more women learned the trick of carding, and the mittens spread farther south. One reason for this was that Hildur Olsson, an ingenious businesswoman from Vittangi, gave a pair to Princess Sibylla. The princess wore her mittens during a royal tour and on a skiing trip to Boden in 1933. This royal sign of approval was certainly noted in Tornedalen. During the depression years of the 1930s, mitten knitting was an extra form of support.

It doesn't take long to knit a pair of Lovikka mittens. You can knit them in an evening, but set aside time for preparatory and finishing work. The mittens become extra soft and fluffy when they're knitted from well-spun yarn and brushed with teasels or a steel brush afterward. Instructions, page 114. Photo: Susanne Pagoldh.

cotton yarn was considered especially elegant.

Men's sweaters had squared necklines and were drawn on over the head. Women's sweaters were cut open into cardigans. A number of Delsbo sweaters from the 1800s have been preserved. Many of these have the date and initials knitted in. The cuff opening, increases, and side seams were all marked with contrasting patterns made from various fabric pieces that were sewn onto the garment.

In other parishes, such as Ljusdal and Järvsö, the patterns were smaller and simpler, and more spread out over a red background. During a recent inventory of costumes in Ljusdal, women's sweaters were found that had green patterns on either blue or black backgrounds. The patterned area of women's sweaters were short (ending just below the breasts) so that its "skirt" could be seen (see photo page 67).

LEG AND FOOTWEAR

In Frostviken in Jämtland, people often went sockless; shoes were worn without stockings even when it was bitterly cold outside. Instead, they filled their shoes with hay, which was considered warmer than wool stockings. Otherwise, half socks were commonly worn during the winter. They had very short cuffs, scarcely reaching the ankle. The half socks were knitted in two-ply yarns spun from coarse leg wool, sometimes blended with goat or human hair. People also wore footless leggings until the 1890s. Knitted stockings didn't become widespread among the peasants until the nineteenth century. Itinerant peddlers sold them, and they became known as West Götaland stockings as a result of the asso-

A red patterned wool sweater is part of Ljusdal's folk costume. Inspired by her own costume, Inger Rosell has designed a better-fitting and more comfortable garment. The colors and the patterns are the same, but the body is longer and the sleeves are wider. Not having gussets, the sleeves on the old models were often narrow and tight-fitting. Here we see Inger Rosell in her newly knitted cardigan together with her daughter Mia in a traditional Ljusdal costume. Instructions for the Ljusdal cardigan are on page 100. Photo: Susanne Pagoldh.

ciation with the peddlers.

When my grandmother, Thea Maria Larson, was a child living at Hällan farm in Överkalix in Norrbotten at the beginning of this century, she wore white or gray wool stockings and stuffed her shoes with hay. At that time, all of the children in Överkalix, even the rich ones, wore shoes with upturned toes stuffed with hay. Without the hay, their feet would have frozen in temperatures as low as –30° C (–22° F). But when Thea Maria had her own children during the 1930s, they wore ski boots and ragg wool socks. She knitted the socks herself with black and white blended wool yarns that she purchased. During the 1930s, only the poorest people had to continue using hay in their shoes.

ÅLAND

The Johansson family sheep graze on Ytternäs by Öster farm outside Mariehamn. Photo: Susanne Pagoldh.

Å LAND IS FORMED by a group of more than 6000 islands and skerries which lie at the juncture of the Baltic Sea and the Gulf of Bothnia. The islands are part of Finland but are self-governing. They are close enough to Sweden that, on a clear day, you can see its contours on the horizon over the waters.

Sea and wind dominate the low, bay-studded islands. Trading, fishing, and seafaring have always been of great importance here, and the location is central to the boat traffic between Sweden and Finland. Many years ago, fur traders came here from the east. Now transport ships with all sorts of goods come to Åland, as well as boatload after boatload of tourists enjoying tax-free tobacco and liquor.

We can be certain that people have been knitting on the islands since at least the seventeenth century because Pastor Boetius Murenius noted in 1648 that a man from Thomos denied having "hit and pinched" a woman while she was knitting. The same priest, writing some years later about a bride's engagement gifts, remarked that an honorable bride should give decent presents and not try to pay the priest with children's or women's stockings. No, only proper men's stockings would do.

Women's stockings were short while the men's were much longer. They went over the knee and were tied with a band below the knee. Soft shoes sewn from sealskin (*själskor*) were worn with thick wool stockings (shoe socks), and in the winter they were also stuffed with hay or straw. Such shoes were worn as late as the 1960s.

The tradition of giving stockings as wedding gifts lasted until the nineteenth century. By then, the bride only needed to knit for the groom, and she lovingly knitted intricate patterns. Otherwise, thick, usually striped, stockings and socks were knitted in red and gray yarn spun from blended wool and linen.

Although Åland's hiding places have been

ransacked once or twice by folk life enthusiasts, and typical old garments were collected by the Finnish-Swedish folk costume collective in Brages, very few mittens and sweaters have been preserved. Perhaps knitting was not considered sufficiently authentic or perhaps *sticksöm,* as it was called, was deposed by crochet, which was considered stylish for women's clothing in the nineteenth century.

Åland's museum has only a few pairs of knitted wool mittens in its collection. Some have little patterns in gray and brown which are similar to the overall-patterned mittens which were knitted on Gotland. Others are gaily colored half mittens. Half mittens, which freed the fingers, were quite useful, especially when fishnets had to be drawn out of the water or the pages of the psalm book turned. On Ecker Island, *nålbinding* mittens were common. Not a single old knitted sweater is to be found at the museum.

CAPS DUG UP FROM GRAVES

When the church in Jomala on Åland (the largest of the islands) was excavated in 1961, a number of skeletons were found in graves under the floor of the church. Mostly women lay in the northern half of the church while more men lay in the south end. Many of the women had bonnets of silk and other fabrics, and the men had leather hats.

But one casket contained a brown-haired woman wearing a red knitted wool cap. The cap had patterns of birds and crowns knitted in black yarn. Red wool knitted stockings covered her feet. A Swedish copper coin dated 1745 lay next to the body. A wool cap knitted with stripes of red, yellow, and blue was found in another grave.

The stockings and both caps are now in Åland's museum. Anne-Marie Rinne-Vest, the museum's textile conservator, has studied these garments and detected a pattern on the cap's inside which was barely visible on the outside. Besides birds, crowns, and hearts, the cap was decorated with triangles and two different flower designs. The smaller flower, which is fragile and twisted and which has both a stalk and leaves, is

reminiscent of the carnations which occur in knitting and weaving patterns in Sweden and Finland. (For more on carnations, see page 13.)

The striped cap is knitted in stockinette with alternating narrow and broad bands. At first glance, it seems to have been badly dyed, but it is possible that the variations in the colors could have been made intentionally. Such "flame" effects result from ikat dyeing, a form of knotted tie-dye in which the yarn is dyed before it is knitted. Ikat-dyed yarn has been used on caps in both Denmark and Sweden.

Now the disinterred caps are tobacco brown and bleached turquoise blue with lighter yellow and darker black, dark green, and wine red sections. Unfortunately, we don't know how they originally looked before lying with their owners for 200 years under the church floor. None of the

Wave- or peacock-patterned wool stockings from Vård Island and Saltvik. Similar patterns have been knitted on stockings in Finland. In Österbotten, the zigzag-patterned stockings are called crooked socks. These stockings are in Åland's museum. Photo: Nils Korpi.

Anne-Marie Rinne-Vest has written instructions for one of the old caps from Jomala. The new version pictured here is knitted in vegetal-dyed yarn. No one is sure what the colors originally were. Instructions, page 116. Photo: Susanne Pagoldh.

This cap was worn by a woman found lying in a casket under the floor in Jomala Church. It wasn't common for women to wear knitted caps in Scandinavia. Now the cap is in Åland's museum in Mariehamn. There is a band with carnations and other flower designs between the black bands with crowns and birds. Photo: Per-Ove Högnäs.

garments has been color-analyzed. Additional colors might have faded away or changed due to chemical processes.

Anne-Marie Rinne-Vest believes that during the 1700s such a fine and well-worked cap would have had red, blue, and green colors from plant dyes. These were colors that were both expensive and difficult to obtain and would therefore be considered elegant. Red could be obtained from madder, blue from indigo or woad (which used to grow wild on Åland), and green from the yellow of birch leaves overdyed with indigo.

Both caps were double-layered—that is, made in a long tube with one half drawn in and serving as the lining for the other. The lining is loosely knitted with thick, undyed yarn.

WOOL AND LINEN YARNS

People have spun knitting yarns from both wool and flax. Flax was grown on the largest and most fertile islands of Åland. Almost everyone had sheep; even the poorest crofters had at least a few ewes.

In the spring, the sheep were taken by boat to an islet where they were left alone to graze. Sheep can swim but don't willingly go into the water; their fleeces quickly become wet and heavy, and so they can't swim very far. After midsummer, the lambs were separated from the ewes. Then the lambs, ewes, and rams were each left on different islands until the first snows came. They were shorn twice a year, in spring and winter.

After the fall slaughter, all the washing, carding, and spinning with the wool began. First, the wool was coarsely carded on a bench or chair carder before it was finely carded on hand cards. Many dark winter evenings were spent working in front of the kitchen fireplace. Those who wanted to or were able to sometimes gathered for a *kardantalka*, or carding bee, at the neighbors'. People from different farms worked together to help one another with carding and spinning and to chat, eat good food, drink coffee, and hear funny stories. Similar get-togethers were held when flax was being processed.

Today there are just over 2500 sheep on the islands, and an Åland wool washing and spinning service has opened up in Hammarland on the large island of Åland. Most of the sheep which graze on the islands and islets are Landrace, a Finnish fine-wool breed. Many sheep farmers still follow the old tradition of taking the sheep in boats to graze on islets from early summer to just before Christmas. If there is enough grass, the wool will be lustrous and fine even if the lambs are rather small.

FINLAND

One of the older buildings in frost-nipped Åbo. Photo: Susanne Pagoldh.

EAST MEETS WEST in Finland. Its knitted sweaters and mittens are imbued with colors and patterns that beckon one eastward. Their colors are stronger and more luminous than in the rest of Scandinavia.

In Nådendal, a little city just north of Åbo, there was a Birgittine cloister which was famous for its stockings and mittens. After the Reformation, when the cloisters lost their large estates, the nuns began to produce stockings and mittens to remain self-supporting. There is some dispute as to whether the garments were knitted or made in *nålbinding*. But most experts agree that stockings were knitted for export from Nådendal starting in the seventeenth century.

During the eighteenth century, Nådendal was a stocking city, and men, women, and children were involved in the craft. Knitting had become such a phenomenon that the city officials forbade knitting in public places—it was considered shameful.

Later on, knitted dolls were a specialty in Nådendal. At the end of the nineteenth century, the dolls were popular souvenirs for the Russian and Finnish socialites who came to the resort town. Dolls are still sold to tourists, but today they are nuns with knitting needles and skeins of yarn.

STOCKINGS FOR LIFE

Traditionally, before marrying, a girl had to have made enough pairs of stockings to last for 20 years or so. Girls became skillful stocking knitters and collected their work in wooden dowry chests. Some girls made enough stockings to last a lifetime.

In Österbotten, as in many other areas in

Scandinavia, it was customary for girls, after they had been confirmed, to sleep outside in sheds or in lofts in the summer. Girls were regarded as mature enough then to have contact with boys. Their textile collections were hung in the sheds ready for inspection when the boys came for nocturnal visits. The richer the farmstead, the more finely "clothed" the girls' shed was. Sheets, hand towels, and skirts hung from the walls and ceiling, and the stockings were hung between the scarves and legging bands.

Sheep were shorn three times a year in Österbotten. The long fall clip was used for knit-ting stockings. Knitted stockings were fulled and hung to dry on blocking boards so that they would be quite tight and warm. Women carded, spun, and knitted for their own family, and knitting stockings was part of the servants' work. When the weather was too miserable for outside work, the maids had to sit inside and knit.

Cotton was a new and fashionable fiber during the nineteenth century, and in many areas of the country, festival and church stockings were knitted in white linen or cotton yarn. In several districts, red-and-white-striped stocking shafts began to be popular. The foot part wasn't visible

The patterns and style of these mittens were taken from a pair of old mittens from Tjöck in south Österbotten. The original mittens, made before the First World War, are in Åbo's provincial museum. They were knitted with lustrous, almost gaudy synthetic colors on a white background. A black ground was also common on this type of mitten. Instructions, page 112. Photo: Susanne Pagoldh.

so it was usually knitted just in white. Red-and-white-striped cotton stockings were also knitted in Sweden.

People wore pattern-knitted stockings, in both wool and cotton, for holiday clothing. In Österbotten, most of the embellished stockings had twisted, scroll, or zigzag striping or checks. Basketweave squares (or birch-bark squares, as the technique of knitting *entrelac* was called) were seen in many parts of Finland but were most common in Tavastland and Österbotten. Black, red, yellow, and green were the preferred colors for *plätta* or *dammspelastrumpona*, as the checked patterns were called.

LEGGINGS

Knitted stockings were common in Finland even in the eighteenth century, but footless leggings, or *benholkar*, were also worn. Sometimes, leggings were worn with shoes stuffed with hay or straw. Another style of footwear stems from the women's tradition of having different kinds of coverings for their legs and feet. The earliest leggings were sewn of fabric, but eventually they were knitted instead. In many cases, the leggings began as stockings. When the stocking feet were worn out, the torn sections were cut away. Today's leg warmers, which are so popular with teenagers, descend from the leggings.

Stockings were impractical for wearing with birch-bark shoes, which used to be worn in east Finland, since the shoes couldn't repel water. For summer wear, leggings were knitted in cotton and linen yarns. The leggings were a good protection for the legs of women working outdoors on the farm; otherwise, they would get scratched up by straw and stubble. For work inside the house, leggings were quite comfortable.

During the winter, women in certain districts wore short socks inside leather-soled birch-bark shoes, wool leggings for the lower legs, and knitted linen knee protectors. Knee protectors and leggings were held up with bands knotted under the knee. These were considered shabby and ugly.

This cotton stocking leg with entrelac, or birch-bark, patterning is from the Kristinestad district in Österbotten. Similar diagonal patchwork stockings were knitted in Norway and Sweden. This stocking leg is in the Swedish-Finnish Textile Archive. Technique described on page 116. Photo: Susanne Pagoldh.

PATTERNED FESTIVAL SWEATERS

The upper classes and some city bourgeois wore knitted sweaters as early as the 1600s. Both men and women wore these garments, which could be bought ready-made or imported. However, it wasn't until well into the nineteenth century that sweaters were worn by the ordinary people out in remote areas of the country.

During the 1830s, both men's and women's sweaters were knitted in Kymmenedalen. They were one-colored or had multicolored zigzag patterns in striking colors. Unfortunately, not a single one of these sweaters remains, but there are many sweaters from Österbotten. Some of these are wool or cotton lice sweaters with patterns on

Ann-Cathrine Wasmuth Ericson has used the designs and patterns from fragments of a man's cotton sweater from Vörå in Österbotten for the child's sweater pictured here. The adult-sized sweater is knitted in a wider, less fitted style than the original, which was from Pörtom and is now in the Swedish-Finnish Textile Archive. Note the placement of the patterns. The Österbotten sweater is reminiscent of Norwegian lice sweaters (see pages 47 and 49), but the patterns go farther up the sleeves. Instructions, pages 90 and 91. Photo: Susanne Pagoldh.

the shoulders and sleeves, and some are the special sweaters from Korsnäs which are both knitted and crocheted. Two-color sweaters with carnation patterns were also knitted in Korsnäs.

The seed-pattern sweaters from Pörtom and Vörå have been made since the end of the nineteenth century. Cotton sweaters were considered finer garments and were reserved for holiday wear. For every day, simple undyed wool sweaters were more suitable. Some of these had simple stripe patterns. Most of the patterned sweaters were knitted for men and boys. Young girls knitted these labor-intensive sweaters as gifts for their fiancés. Similar seed-pattern sweaters were also knitted in other areas of the country.

Part of the reason so much knitting has been preserved from the Swedish-speaking areas is the rich textile tradition in Österbotten. It is also partly due to the Swedish-speaking people's strong interest in folk costumes.

During the years 1928–1935, Hjördis Dahl bicycled from farm to farm in the Swedish villages, collecting textiles for what would become Martha's Handicraft Archive. She worked for Finland's Swedish Martha Collective, a union of Swedish-speaking women. Hjördis searched through attics, sheds, and rag sacks to save what was left of the peasant textiles. She made her tour through the villages just in the nick of time. During the war years which followed soon afterward, many fine wool garments were sold as wool rags. There were a few professional knitters left, but knitting was on the way to becoming a hobby rather than a household necessity.

Now, Martha's Handicraft Archive has a number of samplers and garments. Martha's Archive is the foundation of the Swedish-Finnish Textile Archive in Dragsfjärd in the Åbo archipelago.

This means that anyone interested in handicrafts can come and study and receive inspiration from the collections.

KORSNÄS SWEATERS

A very special type of sweater developed in a little area around Korsnäs in Österbotten. These unique sweaters have both pattern knitting and pattern crocheting. The shoulders, sleeves, and lower edges of the body are crocheted, making those parts form-fitting and inelastic. The other parts are knitted, giving more flexibility around the stomach and elbows. If you think about how much a stomach can change in form and size during a lifetime, then the elasticity is quite important. By the same token, the crocheted sections keep the sweater from stretching out too (right) This cotton knitting sampler is from Pyttis in Nyland and is now in the Swedish-Finnish Textile Archive. Similar cross patterns were knitted on stockings in Estonia. Photo: Kamera-Boden, Åbo.

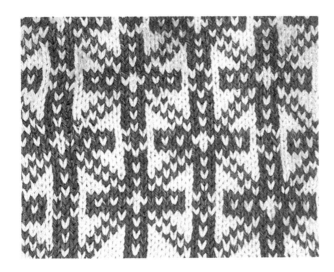 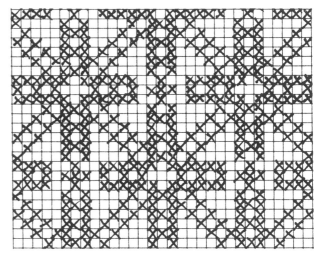

An old patched man's wool sweater from Pörtom in Österbotten was the inspiration for this new sweater. The original was buttoned on the left shoulder and shaped at the waist. The new design is wider and less fitted and knitted with softer and thicker Åland wool yarns. The original sweater is in the Swedish-Finnish Textile Archive. Instructions, page 87. Photo: Susanne Pagoldh.

much. Crocheting also keeps the lower edge from getting wide and unshapely, which can happen to old knitted sweaters that have been washed too often.

The oldest information on Korsnäs sweaters is from 1854. The sweaters have been made and worn in Korsnäs since then without a break except during wartime, when there was a shortage of materials. Gretel Dahlberg, who was born and raised in Töjby (south of Korsnäs), has devoted many years to research on the history of the sweaters and the people who made and wore them. When she was a little girl, she was a frequent visitor to her uncle's and the parish's dyeworks, Frans Lunds. She was fascinated by the dyeworks, and while she sat there together with her mother and female relatives doing handwork, they heard many stories about the colorful sweaters. Her great-grandmother made Korsnäs sweaters, and Gretel has continued the tradition in a more modern way: she teaches courses and has written a book, *Korsnäs Sweaters Then and Now*.

In most of the villages in the Korsnäs district, there were expert workers—women who were specialists in crocheting the color-rich patterns. The master didn't work the knitted parts alone: three or four other knitters would help her. They would sit in a circle with knees touching and knit around on the sweater body. The most expert knitters knitted the seed-pattern rounds while the others did the plain rounds. But some women did all the knitting and crocheting on the sweaters themselves. For a master, this could take about three weeks.

Most of the Korsnäs sweaters were made by women for men. The sweaters were a part of the traditional men's folk costumes in Korsnäs and were worn tucked into trousers under a vest and crocheted suspenders. The suspenders were red and had pattern figures matching those on the sweater edges. Crocheted and patterned tobacco and coin pouches were also part of the costumes. Women also wore these sweaters but didn't usually have the time to knit their own.

Men usually received their sweaters as engagement gifts, but the sweaters might also be given to important people, such as the priest, a teacher, or, as was done at the beginning of this century, to midwives. Aurora Berg usually wore her Korsnäs sweater when she rode out in a sleigh or skied to a place to help bring a new baby into the world. The sweater had been a gift to her from the women of Korsnäs.

No Korsnäs sweater is exactly like another. Gretel Dahlberg compares making one of these sweaters to the creation of a work of art. Those who knit and crochet the sweaters combine traditional patterns and colors with their own ideas. Some sweaters have four colors, while others have six.

One reason that these sweaters are so richly

colored is that Korsnäs has had its own parish dyer since 1854. Ulrik Ingström was the first dyer. Before he opened his dyeworks at Hinikke mill in Korsnäs, he had lived in St. Petersburg for a few years and had learned his trade there. The dye materials, which made so many sweaters and mittens sparkle and glow, came from the large German factories of Bayer Leverkusen and IG Farben.

The knitted sections of the sweaters had seed patterns in red and blue or red and green on a natural white background. The crocheted parts were always red with figures in blue, green, yellow, light red, orange, or lilac. Both wool and cotton yarns were used. Some dyeing was also done at home, with either purchased dye materials or hand-prepared plant materials. The red colors on the old sweaters varied considerably, from red-brown to raspberry. Patterns from the sweaters were also knitted or crocheted on caps and mittens.

Usually these colorful sweaters were worn for festivals and Sundays. When a sweater was worn out, it would be worn under a shirt for heavy work or seal hunting. But Korsnäs sweaters didn't wear out quickly. A good-quality, three-ply wool yarn was handspun for the sweaters. The neck opening was squared, and as deep in the back as in the front so that either side could be worn at the front. If the sweater was turned often, it would wear evenly on all sides. When the lower edges of the body and sleeves eventually did wear out, new edges could be crocheted on. In this way, the sweaters could last for three generations.

The sweaters used to be worn only in Korsnäs, but now anyone who finds them attractive can wear them. The designs have spread to Sweden via weekly magazines and knitting books, and they traveled to the United States with the Österbotten people who emigrated there. Sweaters are also brought by visitors to Korsnäs.

There are still women who knit the sweaters by special order and many who take courses to learn how to make them. Most of Gretel Dahlberg's students are older women, but during the last few years, some younger women have

also become interested in the Korsnäs sweaters.

PRACTICAL MITTENS

When the Finnish winters were at their worst, people often wore two pairs of mittens. There were various types of mittens, either knitted or made in *nålbinding,* in white or gray wool. Another way to fight the cold was to wear knitted wool mittens inside larger skin mittens. Wool

This Korsnäs
(Österbotten)
sweater is partly
knitted and partly
crocheted. Gretel
Dahlberg, who
made the sweater,
also dyed the yarns.
The reds come from
madder and cochi-
neal, yellow from
onion skins, and
green from reeds.
Older Korsnäs
sweaters were dyed
with both synthetic
and natural dyes,
which were occa-
sionally mixed.
Photo: Susanne
Pagoldh.

A wool holiday mit-
ten from Karelia.
The mitten is in
Åbo's provincial
museum. Photo:
Pekka Kujanpää,
1987.

wrist warmers, both patterned and unpatterned, were worn over the gap between the mittens and the lower arm.

Rya mittens were marvelously warm and practical. These wool gauntlets had patterns in a contrasting color scattered over the hand and thumb. Such lice or seed patterns were called bird's-eyes, or *linnunsilmiä* in Finnish. This pattern was simply referred to as seed stitch in the Swedish-speaking parts of Finland, and the mittens were called *rasat* in Virdois in central Finland. On rya mittens, each bird's-eye was made with a length of yarn 8–12 cm (3–5 in) long whose ends hung loose inside the mitten. These yarn lengths made the warming rya "rug" on the inside.

Patterned wool mittens were knitted in many areas. In south Österbotten and Kymmenedalen, the mittens were particularly striking. In Kymmenedalen, the mittens were commonly made as wedding gifts. A great deal of care went into decorating them with checks, latticework, stars, and crosses. In south Österbotten, the mit-

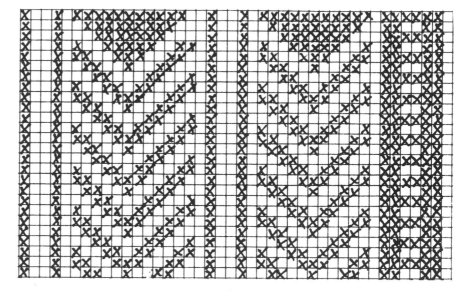

tens showed scrolls of lustrous colors curved around the black or white ground. Bands of birds, flowers, twisted shapes, and garlands surrounded the wrist and hand sections.

Women in the larger towns wore gloves for holidays and holy days, even in warm weather. Summer mittens were white, knitted or made in *nålbinding* with linen, cotton, or wool yarn.

The women's holiday gloves from Karelia had yarn tassels on the fingertips. White, black, or gray wool was used for knitting mittens in southern Karelia. The holiday gloves from the Karelian Isthmus were richly decorated with pattern-knitted stars, roses, and two-end-knitted patterns over the hand and wrist while the fingers were left single-colored.

The Laplanders in Finnish Lapland have known the art of knitting for quite some time. Shoe hay has been replaced by knitted stockings and mittens. Skolt Laplanders, a group who accepted the Greek Orthodox faith, spun sheep's wool on spindles and made their own stockings. Both Skolt and Enare Laplanders wore mittens of natural white wool patterned with two-end knitting or designs in several bright yellow, red, blue, and green shades. These mittens have plaited cords with tassels and look like Swedish Lovikka mittens.

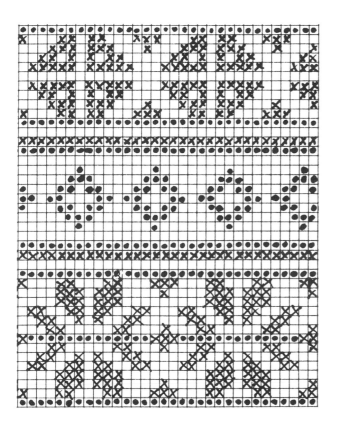

A pattern drawn from an engagement stocking from Wehma in the Egentliga district of Finland. The stockings were knitted in wool with patterns in dark blue on a white ground. The seams are well marked on the back of the leg, and zigzag patterns form wedges as the increases were made for the calf muscles. Such stockings were worn with knee trousers. This garment is in Åbo's provincial museum.

(left) A pattern graphed from a tassel-tipped glove in Åbo's provincial museum (see color picture, p. 78).

PATTERN INSTRUCTIONS

Some of the patterns which follow have been collected from knitters and museums throughout the Nordic countries, while others were developed especially for this book. For this reason, there are some variations in sizing. All of the sweaters marked with an asterisk (*) are knitted following the basic model given below. For all other patterns, the size and measurements are given in the instructions. In the pattern diagrams, 1 square equals 1 stitch.

ABBREVIATIONS

k = knit	cn = circular needle
p = purl	spn = single-pointed needles
st = stitch	cm = centimeter
rnd = round	in = inch
yo = yarn over	g = gram
ssk = slip 2 sts separately to right needle as if to knit, knit these two together through back loops.	nr = metric size
	US = US size
	inc = increase
	dec = decrease
k2 tog = knit 2 together	sc = single crochet
p2 tog = purl 2 together	ch = chain
x = times	hdc = half double crochet
dpn = double-pointed needles	dc = double crochet

CHOOSING YARNS

Yarns are suggested for each pattern, but they may differ slightly from the Scandinavian yarns used in the original garments. Begin by knitting a sample with the suggested yarn and needle size, and check your gauge carefully. If your gauge isn't correct, change needle sizes. Advice on how to check gauge is given below.

Since the weight of different yarns can vary considerably, the quantity of yarn specified for a garment is approximate. It is also difficult to estimate precise amounts of yarn required because everyone knits differently; knitting more tightly or loosely will affect the quantity of yarn used. Variations in the amount of yarn used are also affected by the lengths of stranded yarns in two-color knitting. If you are uncertain about the quantity of yarn needed, ask the yarn shop to hold an extra skein or two of yarn from the same dyelot.

The quality of yarn is very important for the appearance of the garment. A sweater knitted in a smooth, tightly spun yarn will look totally different from one knitted in a soft and fluffy or uneven handspun yarn. Choose yarns appropriate for each type of garment. Soft and fancy yarns which work well for sweaters are inappropriate for socks, which must be hard-wearing and able to withstand multiple washings.

As a rule, the newly designed garments in this book are knitted of thicker and softer yarns than those commonly available in earlier times. We have used only 100 percent wool and cotton yarns.

Good-quality wool is usually more expensive than synthetic yarns but produces better results. It takes only one or two washings to see the great differences between natural and synthetic fibers. Acrylic sweaters become pilled and gray while wool sweaters knitted with high-quality yarn retain their original qualities over time.

WASHING INSTRUCTIONS

All of the garments in this book which use wool yarns must be carefully hand washed with a gentle soap. (This includes the sweater on page 19 which uses a wool/ linen yarn.) Water temperature should be held at about 30° C (86° F). The water temperature itself is not so critical: wool can stand high temperatures if it is heated gradually and cooled slowly. Do not shock it by moving it directly from warm to ice-cold water or agitating it. If you do not want to hand wash woolen garments, choose superwash wool yarns, which can be machine washed.

After washing, the woolen garment should be dried on a flat surface. Hanging wool garments will cause them to stretch and lose their shape.

The cotton yarn used for the Finnish sweater on page 75 can be machine washed in water of 60° C (140° F) water without losing its luster and shape.

GAUGE

Always knit a sample to ensure that your stitch gauge matches that in the pattern instructions. Knitting such a sample will also help you determine whether the colors and patterns will look right.

Knit a sample of at least 15 × 15 cm/6 × 6 in. Count how many stitches and rows you have per 10 cm/4 in. If there are too many stitches and/or rows, the needles are too small—knit another sample with larger needles. If there are too few stitches, the sample is too loosely knitted. Try again with thinner needles.

If the garment is to be knitted on circular needles with patterns in two or more colors, it is important that the sample be knitted in the same manner. One way is to make a tube with sock needles (sets of four or five double-pointed needles) and then cut it so that it can be laid flat and the stitches counted. It doesn't take much yarn to knit samples, and the reward is a well-fitting garment. It's no fun to rip out a half-finished sweater when you suddenly realize that it's too small.

CUTTING KNITTED PIECES

An advantage to knitting a garment on circular needles and then cutting the holes for sleeves and neck is that it is easier to maintain an even gauge throughout. When a sweater knitted in the round is divided into two parts for the armholes and then knitted back and forth on straight needles, the gauge changes slightly. It is also more difficult to knit patterns (especially in two colors) from the purl side.

Cutting knitted pieces is not difficult—just measure carefully before you begin to sew and cut. Sew a double line of stitches by machine so that there is no risk of the knitting's raveling.

Don't forget to allow for a seam allowance on the upper edge of each sleeve—this is especially important on sweaters with color patterns. When all the parts have been knitted, measure the armhole carefully. Baste the sleeves and body together by hand first to check the sleeve position. Mark the position and depth of the armhole with a basting thread in a contrasting color, then remove the sleeves. Stabilize the armhole by machine stitching two closely-spaced rows of straight or zigzag stitches, about 1–1.5 cm/⅜–⅝ in in from the basting line. Then clip the armhole between the sets of seam lines and sew in the sleeve. The sleeve's topmost knit row should lap over the seam line on the inside and be stitched down (a herringbone stitch works well).

The neckhole is clipped in a

similar manner. Measure, baste, and then sew a double seam by machine around the basting line. Don't clip too deeply—cutting away more than 7 cm/2¾ in seldom yields a round neckline. Clip away excess material but leave a seam allowance of at least 1 cm/⅜ in. Sew together the shoulder seams if you have not already done so. It is easier to do the machine stitching around the neck and arm openings if the shoulder seams are left open.

SIZES

There are various ways to determine the correct sizing for garments. One way is to measure the body and then add an allowance for ease in body movement, but how much extra to allow varies considerably from person to person. It also depends on how thick the sweater will be and the weight of the yarn used. A simple way to determine correct sizing is to measure an old sweater of the desired size and of similar weight and yarn size. Be sure to measure the arm length from the back of the neck to the wrist. The sleeves are knitted longer on a small sweater than on a wide one which does not have turned-back cuffs. All measurements given in the instructions refer to the size of the garment and not the body size.

Basic Model

The following sizes for the basic model sweater are used for all patterns marked with an asterisk *:
S = small
M = medium
L = large
Medium size can fit both a man 180 cm (6 ft) tall and of average weight as well as a 14-year-old 160 cm (5 ft, 4 in) tall who likes large sweaters. However, the sleeve length will have to be adjusted somewhat depending on the wearer's arm length.

The sweaters described here are generally fitted and rather short, with straight sewn-in sleeves. If you prefer a below-the-hip length, allow for the extra length.

Ribbing draws in the lower edges of a sweater. How much it draws in depends on the type of ribbing. Wide ribs, for example, k4, p4, draw in rather more than k1, p1 ribbing.

Determining Your Size

The basic model given here uses 3-ply worsted weight Greenland wool yarn, and is knitted on circular needles 4.5 mm/US 7 in two colors (see photograph, page 31). Begin by knitting a gauge sample. The gauge is 20 sts and 22 rows per 10 cm/4 in, or 2 sts and 2.2 rows per cm/5 sts and 5.5 rows per inch.

To determine how many stitches to cast on, multiply the number of stitches per cm/inch times the desired circumference (measured at the bustline).

The drawings show which measurements should be taken from a sweater of similar size laid flat on a table. The width for the front is half the total bust measurement.

For a size *small*, first multiply the front width of a similar sweater by 2 to get the total chest size. For example, 2×55 cm = 110 cm. Using the Greenland wool (2 sts per cm), the total number of stitches needed is 220 (110×2). In inches, 2×21.5 in = 43 in. At 5 sts per in, the total number of stitches needed is 215 (43×5).

For a *medium* sweater, 2×59 cm = 118 cm, and 2 sts per cm $\times$ 118 cm = 236 sts/$2 \times 23¼$ in = 46½ in; 5 sts per in $\times$ 46½ in = 233 sts.

For a size *large*, 2×62 cm = 124 cm; 2 sts per cm $\times$ 124 cm = 248 sts/$2 \times 24½$ in = 49 in; 5 sts per in $\times$ 49 in = 245 sts.

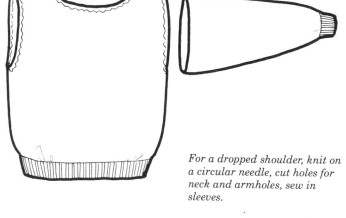

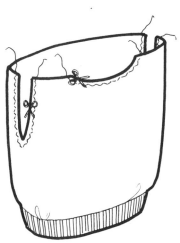

For a dropped shoulder, knit on a circular needle, cut holes for neck and armholes, sew in sleeves.

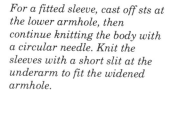

For a fitted sleeve, cast off sts at the lower armhole, then continue knitting the body with a circular needle. Knit the sleeves with a short slit at the underarm to fit the widened armhole.

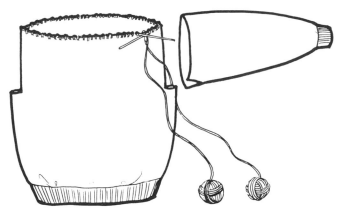

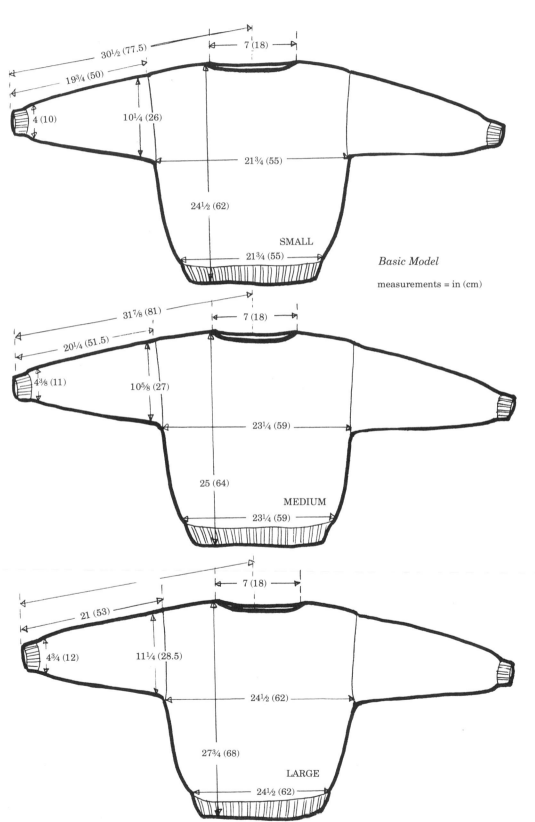

30½ (77.5)

19¾ (50)

7 (18)

4 (10)

10¼ (26)

21¾ (55)

24½ (62)

SMALL

21¾ (55)

Basic Model

measurements = in (cm)

31⅞ (81)

20¼ (51.5)

7 (18)

4⅜ (11)

10⅝ (27)

23¼ (59)

25 (64)

MEDIUM

23¼ (59)

7 (18)

21 (53)

4¾ (12)

11¼ (28.5)

24½ (62)

27¾ (68)

LARGE

24½ (62)

RIBBED EDGING

The ribbing should be knitted on needles one or two sizes smaller than the needles for the body so that the lower edge will not be too loose and roll up. Using the Greenland sweater as an example, cast on 220 (236) (248) sts on cn 3.5 mm/216 (232) (244) on US 5 and rib k1, p1 for 8 cm/3 in. When the ribbing is finished, change to cn 4.5 mm/US 7 and knit one or two rows in one color before beginning the pattern.

ADJUSTING THE PATTERN

The number of stitches required for a pattern repeat will not necessarily fit evenly into the number of stitches required for the garment. When this

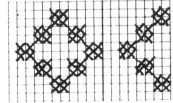

happens you will need to adjust the number of stitches in the garment to an even multiple of the pattern stitches. Usually this adjustment is done with increases rather than decreases, making the garment looser rather than tighter. For example, if a pattern is knitted over 6 stitches and then repeated, and you are knitting a glove with 58 stitches, then increase 2 stitches in a plain area to get to an even multiple of 6 before beginning to knit the pattern area.

SET-IN SLEEVES

The basic model has drop-shoulder sleeves. They are easy to knit and usually look good on broad-shouldered people, but for those who have small shoulders or a large stomach, or who prefer a more tightly fitted sweater, the sleeves can be set in. To adjust the armholes for set-in sleeves, mark the sides and bind off 8 sts for each armhole. To continue circular knitting, on the next rnd, cast on sts over the bound-off sts and continue knitting in the pattern until 26 (27) (28.5) cm/10 (11½) (11) in above the bound-off sts for the armhole.

Set-in sleeves must be knitted a little longer than drop-shoulder ones, and a slit should be made at the upper edge of the sleeve at the armpit to allow the seam allowance to turn back on the inside of the armhole. If you are knitting downward from the shoulder, this slit will be in the 1st rnd; if knitting up from the wrist, it will be on the last rnd—that is, do not join the first or last row.

GUSSET

To give extra width to the armhole, you can knit an underarm gusset, of either a small triangular or rhomboid shape. For an example, see the sweater from Kungshamn on pages 8 and 60.

SHOULDERS

When the body is long enough, count the stitches and mark the sides of the sweater. The neck opening should be approximately one-third of the width (at least 18 cm/7 in and up to 25 cm/10 in for a high rollover collar. Set aside the neck opening stitches on a string or stitch holder.

The shoulder stitches are knitted back and forth, separately on each side and then grafted together after the armhole has been clipped open. Another method for closing the shoulder seam, which is strong and nearly invisible, is to knit together pairs of stitches, one each from the front and back, binding off the resulting stitches in the usual manner.

KNITTING THE SLEEVES FROM THE ARMHOLE DOWN

If you are going to knit the sleeves beginning at the armhole, first calculate how many stitches are needed for the sleeve width at the armhole. For the basic model (the Greenland sweater), size small, the calculation is as follows: 2 × 26 cm (= armhole depth) = 52 cm. 2 sts × 52 = 104 sts. In inches, 2 × 10¼ in = 20½ in. 5 sts × 20½ = 103 sts; round up to 104.

You need 40 sts for the cuff (2 × 10 cm = 20 cm × 2 = 40 sts/2 × 4 in = 8 in × 5 = 40 sts). Therefore, the total number of sleeve stitches decreases from 104 to 40, that is, by 64 stitches.

The decs should occur gradually over 45 cm/17¾ in. 45 × 2.2 rows per cm = 99 rows/17¾ in × 5½ rows per in = 98 rows. To dec 64 stitches over 99 (98) rows, dec 2 sts every third row.

Cast on 104 (108) (114) sts on cn 4.5 mm/US 7. Knit the first 1.5 cm/⅝ in in one color going back and forth as if on straight needles. This edging will be turned in and sewn in the armhole seam. If your garment has set-in sleeves, begin the pattern and continue knitting back and forth for another 2 cm/¾ in before changing to circular knitting.

Knit around in the pattern and work decs into established pattern. Dec 2 sts every 3rd rnd until the sleeve is 43 (44) (46) cm/17 (17¼) (18) in or desired length and at least 40 (44) (50) sts remain. When the sleeve is too small to fit on cn, switch to dpn.

If you shorten the sleeve length to less than the lengths suggested above, you will need to arrive at the desired number of cuff stitches by decreasing the extra ones evenly around a rnd or two before the ribbing. If you want longer sleeves, simply continue knitting without any decs, or make the ribbed cuff longer. Change to dpn 3.5 mm/US 5 and rib k1, p1 for 7 cm/2¾ in. Bind off in ribbing.

KNITTING THE SLEEVES FROM THE WRIST UP

If you are knitting the sleeves from the wrist upward, reverse the instructions for knitting sleeves from the shoulder down.

Cast on 40 (44) (50) sts on dpn 3.5 mm/US 5 and knit ribbing for 7 cm/2¾ in. Change to dpn 4.5 mm/US 7 and knit in pattern. Inc 2 sts every 3rd rnd until the sleeve has 104 (108) (114) sts or until desired length. Change to cn if there are too many sts for the dpn. The last 1–1½ cm/⅜–⅝ in of the sleeve should be knitted in stockinette on straight needles in one color. If the sleeves are to be set in, knit the last 2 cm/¾ in of the pattern on straight needles and continue in that manner with one color and stockinette for 1½ cm/⅝ in. Bind off.

If you want to shorten the sleeve, inc more sts in the first cm/⅜ in after the ribbed cuff and/or in the last 4–5 cm/1½–2 in of the sleeve. This will ensure that you have the proper width for the sleeves. Another way to add sts is to knit an underarm gusset (see page 8).

NECK OPENING

If the opening for the head is sufficiently large (18–25 cm/7–10 in), you don't need to cut a neck opening. The Greenland sweater has a large enough neck hole that it does not need to be cut before knitting the high rollover collar. After the sleeve openings have been clipped open and the shoulder sts bound off, just put the neck sts on dpn 3.5 mm/US 5 (if the neck sts have been bound off, pick up sts with a crochet hook) and rib in k1, p1 ribbing for 12 cm/4¾ in. Bind off in ribbing. (Hint: a crochet hook is useful for picking up sts around a neck or sleeve opening that has been clipped open.)

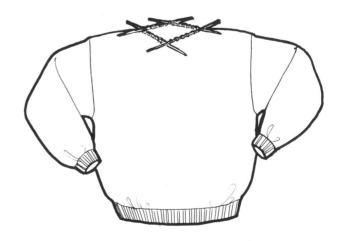

Faroese Sweater *

Photo page 27
Size: S (M) (L)
Yarn: 3-ply worsted weight wool yarn in two colors, approximately 400 g/14 oz of each
Needles: Cn 80 cm, 3.5 mm and 4.5 mm/32 in, US 5 and 7; 40 cm, 4.5 mm/16 in, US 7; dpn 3.5 mm and 4.5 mm/US 5 and 7
Gauge: 20 sts and 20 rows = 10 cm/4 in

The entire sweater is knitted in the round. The sleeves are knitted from the cap and sewn in.

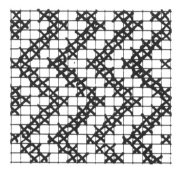

Body: Cast on 220 (236) (248) sts on longer cn 3.5 mm/US 5 and work in k1, p1 ribbing for 7 cm/2¾ in. Change to cn 4.5 mm/US 7 and knit 1 rnd in the main color and then continue in the pattern according to the diagram until the piece measures 36 (37) (40) cm/14 (14½) (15) in. Mark the sides of the sweater and bind off 6 sts on each side for the armholes. Continue knitting in the round. When the piece measures 62 (64) (68) cm/ 24½ (25) (26½) in, put the center 50 sts of both front and back on a string. Bind off the remaining sts.
Sleeves: Cast on 106 (110) (114) sts with the dark color on the shorter cn 4.5 mm/US 7 and, working back and forth as if on straight needles, knit 3 rows in a single color and then 3 rows in pattern. Knit in the round in the pattern according to the diagram and dec 1 st every first, second, and third—but not fourth—rnd until you have 40 (44) (46) sts left. (Change to dpn when neces-

sary.) Knit 1 rnd in a single color and change to dpn 3.5 mm/US 5. Work in k1, p1 ribbing for 8 cm/3 in. Bind off.

Cut open the armholes (see page 81) and sew in the sleeves. Sew the shoulder seams.
High rollover collar: Pick up the neck sts on dpn 3.5 mm/US 5 and work in k1, p1 ribbing for 13 cm/5 in. Bind off in ribbing.

Greenland Sweater *

Photo page 31
Size: S (M) (L)
Yarn: 3-ply worsted weight wool yarn, 900 g/32 oz in two colors
Needles: Cn 80 cm, 3.5 mm and 4.5 mm/32 in, US 5 and 7; dpn 3.5 mm and 4.5 mm/ US 5 and 7
Gauge: 20 sts and 22 rows = 10 cm/4 in

The sweater is knitted in the round, and the armholes are cut open. The sleeves are knitted from the top down and sewn in. See the instructions for the basic model, for which this sweater was used as an example. Variations of the sweater are also detailed in that section.
Body: Cast on 220 (236) (248) sts on cn 3.5 mm/US 5 and work in k1, p1 ribbing for 8 cm/3 in. Change to cn 4.5 mm/US 7 and knit one single-color rnd, increasing 8 (4) (4) sts evenly in the rnd. Knit in pattern accord-

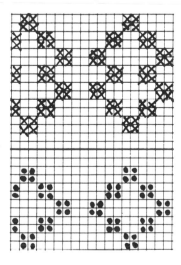

ing to the diagram until the piece measures 62 (64) (68) cm/24½ (25) (26½) in. Mark the sides and then mark the center 25 cm/ 10 in of both front and back for the neck opening. Set these sts aside and then bind off the shoulder sts.
Sleeves: Cast on 104 (108) (114) sts on cn 4.5 mm/US 7. Knit 1–1½ cm/⅜–⅝ in back and forth in stockinette st. Begin knitting in the round in the pattern. Dec 2 sts every 3rd rnd until the sleeve measures 43 (44) (46) cm/17 (17½) (18) in and 40 (44) (50) sts are left. Adjust the pattern as necessary and change to dpn when there are too few sts for cn. Change to dpn 3.5 mm/US 5 and work in k1, p1 ribbing for 8 cm/3 in. Bind off.

Cut open the armholes (see page 81) and sew in the sleeves.
High rollover collar: Pick up the neck sts and work in k1, p1 ribbing for 12 cm/4¾ in. Bind off in ribbing.

Setesdal Sweater *

Photo page 47
Instructions written by Merete Lütken
Size: S (M) (L)
Yarn: 3-ply wool yarn at about 1000 yd/lb, 250 g/9 oz white and 450 g/16 oz black
Needles: Cn 80 cm, 3 mm and 3.5 mm/32 in, US 3 and 5; 40 cm, 3 mm and 3.5 mm/16 in, US 3 and 5; spn 3 mm and 3.5 mm/US 3 and 5.
Gauge: 25 sts = 10 cm/4 in
The sweater is knitted in the round, and the armhole is cut open. The sleeves are knitted in the round from the top down. The front of the sweater may be cut open for a cardigan, and both the front edges and cuffs may be decorated with embroidery.
Note: To obtain an even and pleasing result when joining yarn, overlap ends by 15 cm/6 in. You can make extra-smooth and almost invisible joins by removing one ply from each end and overlapping the remaining yarn.

Body: With white, cast on 288 (296) (304) sts on cn 3 mm/US 3 and knit 9 rnds in k4, p4 ribbing. Then work 10 rnds in p4, k4 ribbing to form a checkerboard. Continue in stockinette until the piece measures 13 (14) (15) cm/5 (5½) (6) in. Change to cn 3.5 mm/US 5 and

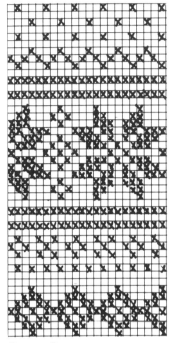

Pattern I

knit pattern I. In the lower part of the body, the pattern is knitted with black on a white background, and the rest of the sweater is knitted in white on a black background. When all of pattern I has been knitted, change back to 3 mm/US 3 needles. Knit lice pattern (a single stitch of a contrasting color every fourth st) on every other rnd following the diagram until the piece measures 44 (46) (50) cm/17¼ (18) (19¾) in. Change to needles 3.5 mm/US 5 and knit pattern II, which ends with 1 rnd in white. Then, with black, knit 1 rnd, purl 1 rnd, knit 3 rnds. Bind off. Mark the sides: there are 144 (148) (152) sts each on the back and front.
Sleeves: Cast on 3 sts in black and knit a triangle in stockinette by increasing 1 st at each

Pattern II

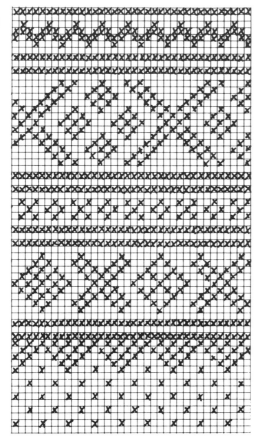

Pattern IV

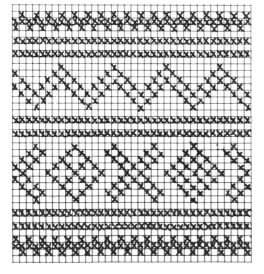

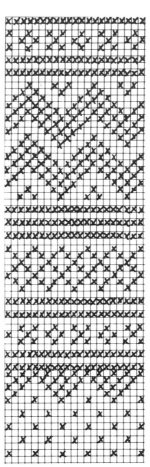

Pattern III

side every third row until there are 15 sts on the needle. Work 2 rows and then dec 1 st at each side. Put these 13 sts on a spare needle.

With black, cast on 135 (138)

(144) sts on shorter cn 3 mm/US 3 and knit 6 rows back and forth in stockinette. Now, put the 13 sts from the spare needle the pattern, dec 2 sts every 7th rnd by ssk on the 2 sts before

onto the cn and knit around for 3 rnds. Change to cn 3.5 mm/US 5 and knit pattern III, working the diagram from the top down. Mark the center st of the triangle and keep it as the center st during the decs. Counting from the first row of the center, knit the center st, and then k2 tog.

Change to cn 3 mm/US 3 and knit in lice pattern on every other rnd, according to the diagram. When the work measures 32 (34) (36) cm/ 12½ (13½) (14¼) in, change back to 3.5 mm/US 5 needles and knit pattern IV from the top down. When that is done, change back to 3 mm/US 3 needles and at the same time dec as follows: k2, k2 tog around: 48 (50) (52) sts. Work in k1, p1 ribbing for 5 cm/2 in. Bind off.

Assembly: Weave in all loose threads. Position each sleeve and baste a cutting line on the

body for the armhole, then machine stitch a double line on each side of the basting and cut the opening. The opening for the sleeves plus gusset will be about 31 (32) (33) cm/12¼ (12½) (13) in. Leaving 25 cm/10 in for the neck opening, sew the shoulders together by turning under the edge at the purl row and grafting the shoulders together. Turn the work to the wrong side and sew down the turned-in facing from shoulder to shoulder.

Turn under the sleeve facing and pin it down. Baste the sleeves to the body with the gusset pointed down so that its edge covers the machine stitching. Working from the right side of the sweater, sew in the sleeves by hand. Sew down the facing on the inside so that all the machine sts are hidden.

If you want a slit at the neck opening, you can sew on a placket and standup collar of heavy woolen fabric as shown in the photo on page 47. With contrasting thread, mark the placement and length of the desired front opening. Cut a piece of woolen fabric for the front placket 3 cm/1 in longer than the thread mark and 20 cm/8 in wide. Place the right side of the placket piece on the wrong side of the front sweater piece, centering it on the mark and with the top edges even. Baste in place, then machine stitch a long V around the marking thread. Cut between the machine stitched lines, and turn the placket to the front. Turn under the sides and the bottom edge of the woolen placket piece, and sew down by hand.

Cut two collar pieces following the pattern. Sew the layers right sides together, clip the curves, turn right side out, and press. Lay the collar on the sweater. Mark the neck edge on the sweater and machine stitch to stabilize it, then trim off excess knitted fabric. Pin on the collar and sew it on by hand. Embroider the collar and placket if desired. The opening can be held together with a clasp.

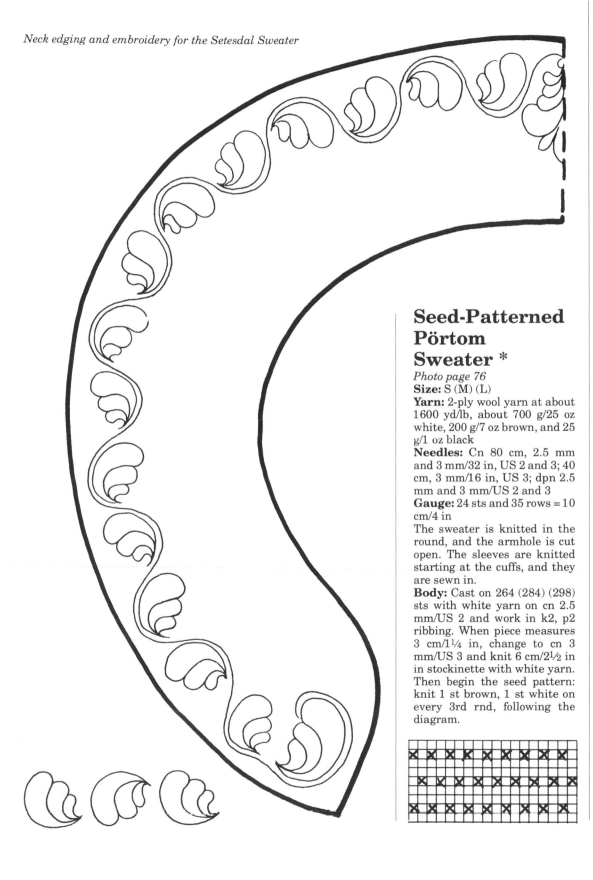

Neck edging and embroidery for the Setesdal Sweater

When the length measures 55 (57) (61) cm/21½ (22½) (24) in, mark the sides of the sweater. Set aside the center 38 sts of the front on a stitch holder. Working back and forth on the rest of the sts, bind off 1 st on each side of the neck edge on the following 2 rows.

When the piece measures 57 (59) (63) cm/22½ (23¼) (24¾) in, knit the shoulders using pattern A. When the work measures 60 (62) (66) cm/23½ (24½) (26) in, set aside the middle 40 sts of the back on a stitch holder. To begin back neck shaping, bind off 1 st on each side of the neck edge on the following 2 rows, working each side separately. When you have finished knitting pattern A and the whole piece measures 62 (64) (68) cm/24½ (25¼) (26¾)

Seed-Patterned Pörtom Sweater *

Photo page 76
Size: S (M) (L)
Yarn: 2-ply wool yarn at about 1600 yd/lb, about 700 g/25 oz white, 200 g/7 oz brown, and 25 g/1 oz black
Needles: Cn 80 cm, 2.5 mm and 3 mm/32 in, US 2 and 3; 40 cm, 3 mm/16 in, US 3; dpn 2.5 mm and 3 mm/US 2 and 3
Gauge: 24 sts and 35 rows = 10 cm/4 in

The sweater is knitted in the round, and the armhole is cut open. The sleeves are knitted starting at the cuffs, and they are sewn in.

Body: Cast on 264 (284) (298) sts with white yarn on cn 2.5 mm/US 2 and work in k2, p2 ribbing. When piece measures 3 cm/1¼ in, change to cn 3 mm/US 3 and knit 6 cm/2½ in in stockinette with white yarn. Then begin the seed pattern: knit 1 st brown, 1 st white on every 3rd rnd, following the diagram.

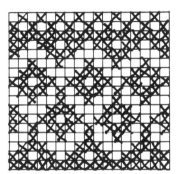

Pattern A

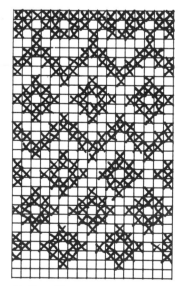

Pattern B

in, bind off the remaining sts.
Sleeves: With white yarn, cast on 48 (52) (60) sts on dpn 2.5 mm/US 2 and work 8 rnds in k2, p2 ribbing. Change to dpn 3 mm/US 3. Begin pattern B. Inc 2 sts every 4th rnd, placing 1 knit st between the incs. (The incs should be worked into the pattern.)

Continue increasing 2 sts every 4th rnd and work in seed pattern until the sleeve has 126 (132) (138) sts. Change to cn 3 mm/US 3 when there are too many sts on the dpn. When the sleeve measures 48 (49) (51) cm/19 (19¼) (20) in, knit pattern C. Finish knitting with 1.5 cm/¾ in worked back and forth in brown yarn. Bind off.

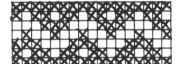

Pattern C

× = brown   • = black

Pattern D

Neck edge: Pick up 128 sts with dpn 3 mm/US 3 and knit the checkerboard in pattern D. Change to dpn 2.5 mm/US 2 on the 13th rnd. Using white yarn, finish the neckline with 8 rnds in k2, p2 ribbing. Bind off in ribbing.

Ullared Sweater *

Photo page 57
Size: S (M) (L)
Yarn: 2-ply wool yarn at about 1600 yd/lb, about 350 g/13 oz each black and rust red
Needles: Cn 80 cm, 2.5 mm and 3 mm/32 in, US 2 and 3; 40 cm, 3 mm/16 in, US 3; dpn 2.5 mm and 3 mm/US 2 and 3
Gauge: 30 sts and 32 rows = 10 cm/4 in

The sweater is knitted in the round. The armholes are cut open and the sleeves are sewn in. The sleeves are knitted starting at the lower edge.
Body: Cast on 334 (356) (372) sts on cn 2.5 mm/US 2. Work in k3, p1 ribbing for 7.5 cm/3 in. Work the ribbing in stripes with rust red and black yarn.

Change to cn 3 mm/US 3 and stockinette st. Mark the sides of the sweater for placement of the side stripe. Knit pattern A (9 rnds). Don't forget the 6 sts for the side stripe. Then knit pattern C. Widen the side stripe to 10 sts on each side of the 2 rust red middle sts, following the diagram. When the whole piece measures 40 (42) (46) cm/15¾ (16½) (18) in, knit the date and initials on the center 30 sts of the front (see diagram).

When the work measures 56.5 (58.5) (62.5) cm/22¼ (23) (24½) in, knit 1 rnd in black. Set aside the center 45 (47) (49) sts of the front on a stitch holder. Keep the back sts on the cn. Knit the shoulders, working back and forth on dpn 3 mm/US

3. Knit pattern A, then pattern B. Dec 1 st on each side of the neck edge every third row

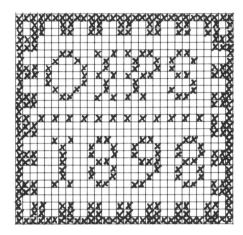

Pattern C

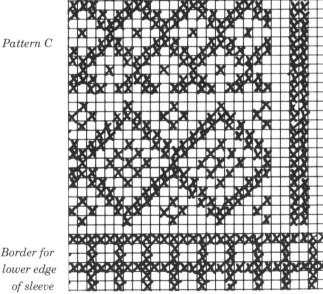

Border for lower edge of sleeve

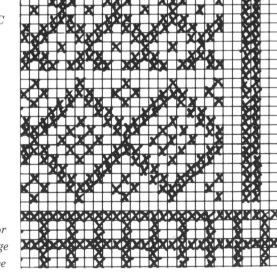

Pattern C

Pattern A

Side stripe pattern for the body

(twice). When the shoulders measure 5.5 cm/2¼ in, cast on 49 (51) (53) sts between the shoulder sts and continue the pattern as on the front side. Bind off the front and back side sts together with an additional needle.

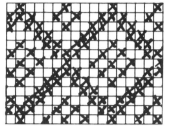

Pattern B

Sleeves: Cast on 76 sts on dpn 2.5 mm/US 2 and knit around with rust red for 4 cm/1½ in. This 4-cm section will be turned under later as a lining for the lower sleeve edge. Now, knit the sleeve border together with the 6-st side stripe (2 sts black, 2 sts rust red, 2 sts black). Knit 1 rnd with rust red, increasing to 84 sts evenly spaced. Change to dpn 3 mm/US 3, knit pattern C, and inc 2 sts (1 st on each side of the knit st at center of the side stripe) every 4th rnd until the sleeve has 154 (157) (165) sts. Change to cn when the sleeve is too wide for dpn. When the sleeve measures 50 (51) (53) cm/19¾ (20) (21) in, knit 2 rnds in black. Dividing the piece at the side stripe, knit in black back and forth for 1.5 cm/⅝ in. Bind off all sts loosely. The black edge will be turned over the armhole seam during assembly.

On the body, machine stitch on both sides of the side stripe pattern to the right depth for the sleeve, and cut it open for the armhole (see page 81). Sew the sleeve in by hand. Turn under and sew the lining at the lower edge of the sleeves. Turn under the black facing on the inside and sew it down to cover the machine stitching.

Neck: Using rust red yarn and dpn 2.5 mm/US 2, pick up about 140 (150) sts along the neck opening and work k1, p1 ribbing for 4.5 cm/1¾ in. Bind off in ribbing. Turn the ribbed edge under and sew it down.

Spjäll (Gusset) Sweater *

Photo page 60
Size: S (M) (L)
Yarn: 2-ply wool yarn at about 1600 yd/lb, approximately 350 g/13 oz each blue and red
Needles: Cn 80 cm, 2.5 mm and 3 mm/32 in, US 2 and 3; 40 cm, 3 mm/16 in, US 3; dpn 2.5 and 3/US 2 and 3
Gauge: 30 sts and 32 rows = 10 cm/4 in
The body of the sweater is knitted in the round; the armholes are cut open and the sleeves are knitted directly from the body. The ribbing at the lower edge is knitted onto the bottom of the body.
Body: Using blue yarn, cast on 332 (356) (372) sts on cn 3 mm/US 3. Mark the sides of the sweater for the placement of the side stripe. Using red and blue yarns, knit in stockinette st, following diagram A. Don't forget the 6 sts of the side

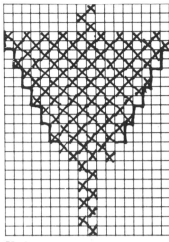

Underarm gusset

stripe. When the work measures 29.5 (31) (33.5) cm/11½ (12¼) (13¼) in, begin the underarm gusset, increasing 1 st on each side of the gusset every other rnd until the whole piece measures 35.5 (37) (39.5) cm/14 (14½) (15½) in and the gusset

is 18 sts wide and about 6 cm/2½ in long. Work the 6 sts of the side stripe into the checkerboard pattern of the gusset (see diagram), and continue knitting pattern A on the body as you knit the gusset.

Set aside the gusset sts on a stitch holder. Continue knitting the body in pattern A and cast on 6 sts over the gusset (these 6 sts are worked in the side stripe pattern).

When the work measures 55 (57) (61) cm/21¾ (22½) (24) in, knit 1 rnd in red and 1 rnd in blue. Mark the center sts of the front and the back. These sts will be the starting point for the diagonal pattern on the shoulders.

Knit pattern B for 3.5 cm/1½ in. Bind off all sts loosely.

Using a crochet hook and blue yarn, pick up 330 (354) (371) sts around the lower edge of the body. Using cn 2.5 mm/US 2, work in k3 blue, p3

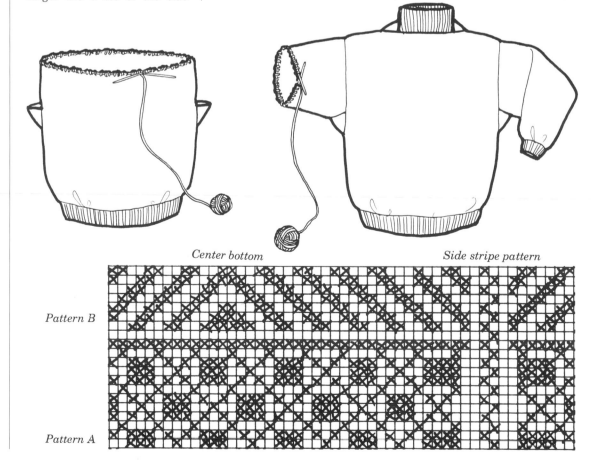

Center bottom   *Side stripe pattern*

Pattern B

Pattern A

red for 3.5 cm/1½ in. Bind off, using red and blue alternately, making a red-blue plaited edging.

Machine stitch a double line on each side of the side stripe's center 4 sts from the shoulder to the sts cast on above the gusset. Cut open between the rows of stitching. Mark the center one-third of the shoulder opening for the neck opening. Machine stitch the shoulder seam from the shoulder to 2 in from the mark for the neck opening. A gusset will fill the 2 in closest to the neck at the shoulder.

Sleeves: Using a crochet hook and red and blue yarn, pick up 1 st for each st of the armhole plus the gusset sts, taking up 160 (168) (174) sts or however many are needed for the pattern. Put the sts on shorter cn 3 mm/US 3, and knit the sleeve. Knit around in pattern A and work the 6 sts of the side stripe pattern centered over the gusset. Dec 2 sts every 4th rnd (1 st on each side of the side stripe pattern) until the sleeve measures 46 (47.5) (49) cm/18 (18¾) (19¼) in and has at least 84 sts.

Knit 2 rnds with blue and dec to 72 (78) (84) sts. Change to dpn 2.5 mm/US 2 and work in k3 red, p3 blue ribbing for 4 cm/1½ in. Bind off alternately with red and blue.

Neck: Pick up 6 sts for the gusset on the side of the neck between the front and back. Knit 2 red, 2 blue (center), 2 red. With a crochet hook, pick up a blue st on the edge, turn and purl back. Pick up a new blue st on the other edge, turn and repeat. Continue knitting in this way, making a stockinette striped gusset for the neck opening. When the gusset has 22 sts, set them aside on a stitch holder and make the gusset on the opposite side of the neck.

Using dpn 2.5 mm/US 2, pick up about 160 sts around the neck, including the gusset sts. Work a high rollover collar in k1, p1 ribbing with red yarn. When the neck measures 12 cm/4¾ in, bind off in ribbing.

Cotton Pörtom Sweater *
Photo page 75
Size: S (M) (L)
Yarn: 4-ply mercerized cotton yarn at about 1600 yd/lb, 500 g/18 oz unbleached white, 100 g/4 oz red, 100 g/4 oz blue
Needles: Cn 80 cm, 2 mm and 2.5 mm/32 in, US 1 and 2; 40 cm, 2.5 mm/16 in, US 2; dpn 2 mm and 2.5 mm/US 1 and 2
Gauge: 35 sts and 40 rows = 10 cm/4 in

The sweater is knitted in the round and cut open for the sleeves. The sleeves are knitted in the round starting at the cuffs and sewn in.

Body: With unbleached white yarn and cn 2 mm/US 1, cast on 384 (412) (432) sts. Work in k2, p2 ribbing for 2 cm/¾ in. Change to cn 2.5 mm/US 2 and knit 9 cm/3½ in in stockinette

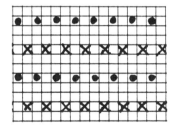

with white yarn. Then begin the pattern. Knit the seed-pattern sts in red and blue yarn, following the diagram until the whole piece measures 54 (56) (60) cm/21¼ (22) (23½) in.

Mark the sides of the sweater and set aside the center 56 sts of the front on a stitch holder or string. Bind off 1 st on each side of the neck opening 3x. Continue knitting back and forth on the cn from one side of the neck opening across the back to the other side of the neck.

When the work measures 56 (58) (62) cm/22 (23) (24½) in, begin the shoulder pattern, which is knitted back and forth on the cn. When the shoulder pattern is finished, bind off the shoulder sts with white yarn.

Sleeves: With two strands of red yarn, cast on 70 (77) (88) sts on dpn 2 mm/US 1, twisting on

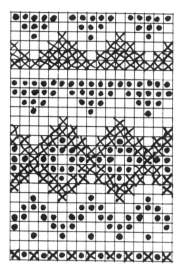

Upper sleeve pattern

Shoulder pattern

every st. This will make a stronger edge than will working with one strand of yarn. Change to a single strand and knit the sleeve border, following the diagram. Change to dpn 2.5 mm/US 2 on the 19th rnd and inc 6 sts.

Continue following the diagram, increasing 2 sts every 3rd rnd on each side of the marked center st where the rnd changes. When the sleeve has 182 (189) (200) sts and measures 47 (48) (50) cm/18½ (19) (19¾) in, knit the upper sleeve pattern, following the diagram. Knit 1 rnd in red and then work back and forth with red for 1.5 cm/¾ in. This edge will be turned under to hide the seam. Bind off loosely.

Assembly: Mark and sew around the armhole (see page 81). Cut the armholes open and sew in the sleeves by hand. Fold the red facing over the machine stitching on the inside of the armhole and hand stitch in place.

Neck: With blue yarn and dpn 2 mm/US 1, pick up 192 sts. Work k2, p2 ribbing for 1 cm/½ in. Bind off.

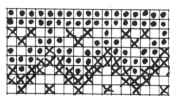

Sleeve (lower edge) patterns

Fisherman Sweater in Linen or Hair-Blend Yarn

Photo page 19
Instructions written by
Carina and Susanne Pagoldh
Size: S (M) (L)
Yarn: 2-ply heavy worsted wool yarn, 600 g/21 oz, and line flax, hair, or linen thread, 200 g/7 oz
Needles: Spn 3 mm and 4/US 3 and 6
Gauge: 17 sts and 23 rows = 10 cm/4 in

The sweater is knitted back and forth on straight needles and sewn together.

The linen is blended with the yarn by taking a few strands of the line flax and knitting them together with the yarn. Don't bother trying to count out an exact number of flax fibers each time. The sweater will look a little uneven and fluffy. Join the flax strands by overlapping them.

Front: Using only the wool yarn (we don't want flax in the ribbing) and spn 3 mm/US 3, cast on 82 (90) (96) sts. Work k1, p1 ribbing for 6 cm/2½ in. Change to 4 mm/US 6 needles and work 4 rows stockinette of wool yarn alone. Then begin blending in the flax. Continue in stockinette, increasing 1 st every 6th row until the piece has 94 (100) (106) sts. When the front measures 37 (38) (40.5) cm/14½ (15) (16) in, bind off 2, 1, 1, 1 sts on each side for the armhole.

When the armhole measures 20 (21) (22.5) cm/8 (8¼) (9) in, bind off for the neck opening. Set aside the center 26 sts on a string or stitch holder and knit each shoulder separately. Bind off 1 st on each side of the neck opening on each of the next 2 rows. When the armhole measures 23 (24) (25.5) cm/9 (9½) (10) in, bind off 1 st at the shoulder every other row until the whole piece measures 62 (64) (68) cm/24½ (25¼) (26¾) in. Bind off, using wool yarn alone.

Back: Work the same as the front until the piece measures 61 (63) (67) cm/24 (24¾) (26¼) in. Set aside the center 28 sts on a string or stitch holder. On the next row, bind off 1 st on each side of the neck opening. Bind off.

High Rollover Collar: Don't use any flax in the neck. Using wool yarn and 3 mm/US 3 needles, pick up about 112 sts.

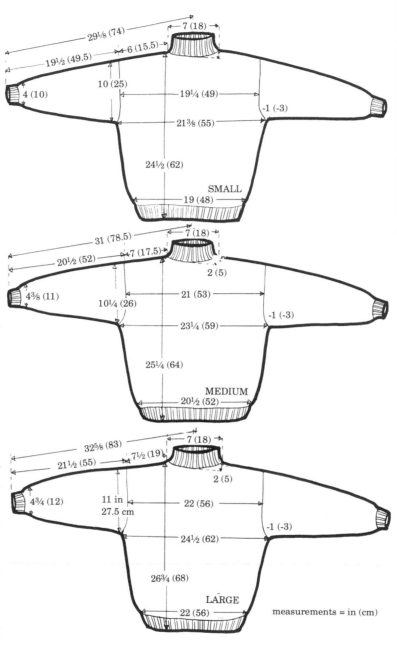

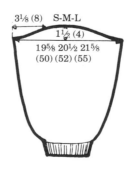

measurements = in (cm)

Work k1, p1 ribbing for 12 cm/4¾ in. Bind off in ribbing.
Sleeves: Using only wool yarn and spn 3 mm/US 3, cast on 34 (38) (42) sts. Work k2, p2 ribbing for 10 cm/4 in. Change to 4 mm/US 6 needles and work in stockinette with flax blended in. Inc 4 sts evenly divided around the 1st row. Then inc 1 st at each side every 4th row until the sleeve has 84 (88) (94) sts. When the sleeve measures 52 (54.5) (57.5) cm/20½ (21½) (22½) in, bind off 2, 1, 1, 1 sts on each side for the armhole. When the whole sleeve measures 56 (58.5) (61.5) cm/22 (23) (24¼) in, bind off all sts. Assemble the sweater with hand stitching.

Child's Sweater with Patterns from Vörå

Photo page 75
Instructions written by Ann-Cathrine Wasmuth Ericson
Size: 6 to 12 months (2 years) (4 years) (6 years)
Width: 50 (60) (64) (68) cm/19½ (23½) (25¼) (26¾) in
Length: 30 (32) (36) (40) cm/11¾ (12½) (14¼) (15¾) in
Yarn: 4-ply mercerized cotton yarn at about 1600 yd/lb. For 6 to 12 months, use about 150 g/6 oz unbleached white and 50 g/2 oz blue; for 2 years, use about 150 g/6 oz white and 100 /4 oz blue; for 4 years, use about 250 g/9 oz white and 100 g/4 oz blue; for 6 years, use about 300 g/11 oz white and 100 g/4 oz blue.
Needles: Cn 40 cm, 2 mm and 2.5 mm/16 in, US 0 and 2; dpn 2 mm and 2.5 mm/US 0 and 2
Gauge: 32 sts and 44 rows = 10 cm/4 in

The child's sweater is knitted in the round, and the armholes and neck are cut open. The sleeves are knitted starting at the cuffs and sewn in.
Body: Using cn 2 mm/US 0 and unbleached white yarn, cast on 160 (192) (204) (224) sts. Work in k2, p2 ribbing for 8 (8) (12) (12) rnds. Change to cn 2.5 mm/US 2. Continue knitting with white yarn and knit in stocki-

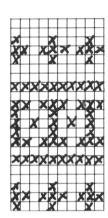

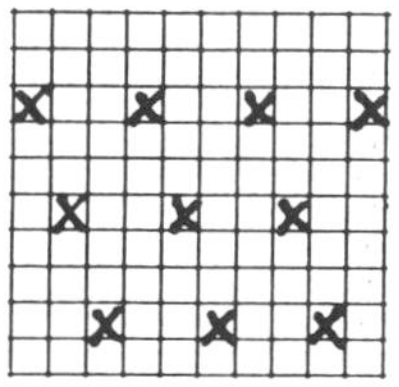

Lice pattern

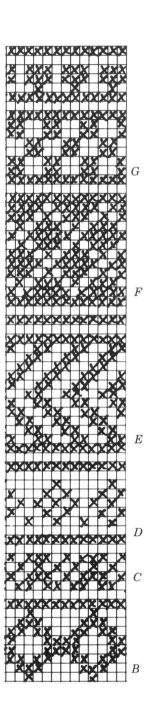

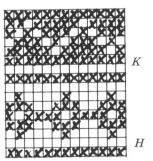

A

B

C

D

E

F

G

H

K

nette st for 2 cm/¾ in. Begin pattern A (about 4 cm/1½ in). Knit 1 cm/½ in in white and then begin the lice pattern, following the diagram for 10 (11) (11) (15) cm/4 (4¼) (4¼) (6) in. After the lice pattern is completed, knit the patterns for the various sizes: C D E G H (C D E G H) (B C D E F G H) (B C D E F G H). Knit until the piece measures 30 (32) (36) (40) cm/ 11¾ (12½) (14¼) (15¾) in and bind off all sts.

Sleeves: Using unbleached white yarn and dpn 2 mm/US 0, cast on 52 (64) (64) (64) sts and work k2, p2 ribbing for 8 (8) (12) (12) rnds. Change to dpn 2.5 mm/US 2. Knit in stockinette with unbleached white yarn for 1.5 cm/½ in. For 6 to 12 months (2 years) sizes, inc 1 st on each side of the knit st at the center every 6th rnd until there are 64 (77) sts. For 4 years (6 years) sizes, inc 1 st on each side of the knit st at the center every 4th rnd until there are 90 (96) sts. Knit the patterns BG (BG) (BFG) (BFG) and then about 2 cm/¾ in lice pattern, then pattern K. Continue knitting in lice pattern for 10 (12) (13) (17) cm/4 (4¾) (5) (6¾) in. When the

sleeve measures 20 (22) (26) (30) cm/8 (8½) (10¼) (11¾) in, knit 1.5 cm/½ in back and forth with unbleached white yarn. Bind off all sts.

Assembly: Weave in all loose threads. Press lightly on the wrong side and baste around the areas marked for the arm

and neck openings. Machine stitch the seams and cut open (see page 81). Cut open the neck either with or without a front slit. You can also cut open one shoulder and sew on buttons. In that case, add a ribbed edging to each side of the shoulder, working 3 buttonholes over 3 sts.

Round neck opening: Pick up about 80 (101) (115) (115) sts around the neck opening beneath the machine stitching and work k1, p1 ribbing for 8 (8) (12) (12) rnds. Bind off all sts.

Lopi Sweater

Photo page 40
Instructions from Alafoss
Size: 34–36 (38–40) (42–44) (48–50) (52–54)
Chest: 94 (98) (103) (107) (111) cm/37 (38½) (40½) (42) (43½) in
Yarn: Bulky weight wool singles at about 600 yd/lb
Main color: 500 (500) (600) (600) (600) g/18 (18) (21) (21) (21) oz
Color 1: 200 (200) (200) (200) (300) g/7 (7) (7) (7) (11) oz
Color 2: 100 (100) (100) (100) (100) g/4 (4) (4) (4) (4) oz
Needles: cn 80 cm, 4.5 mm and 6 mm/32 in, US 7 and 9; 40 cm, 6 mm/16 in, US 9; dpn 4.5 mm/US 7
Gauge: 14 sts and 20 rows = 10 cm/4 in
The sweater is knitted in the round with the sleeves knitted together with the yoke. The sweater is seamless except for sewing down the neck edge.

Body: With color 1 and cn 4.5 mm/US 7, cast on 120 (124) (130) (136) (140) sts. Work in k1, p1 ribbing for 5 (5) (6) (6) (7) cm/2 (2) (2½) (2½) (2¾) in. Change to cn 6 mm/US 9 and work in stockinette st. On the 1st rnd, inc to 132 (138) (144) (150) (156) sts evenly spaced around. Knit pattern I, then continue in stockinette with the main color until the piece measures 40 (41) (43) (45) (46) cm/15¾ (16) (17) (17¾) (18) in. Set aside 9 (9) (10) (10) (10) sts on a string for each armhole. Put the body aside for now.

Sleeves: Using color 1 and dpn 4.5 mm/US 7, cast on 30 (30) (32) (34) (36) sts. Work in k1, p1 ribbing for 5 (5) (6) (6) (7) cm/2 (2) (2½) (2½) (2¾) in. Change to cn 6 mm/US 9 and continue working in stockinette st. On the 1st rnd, inc to 42 (42) (48) (48) (48) sts evenly spaced around. Knit pattern I, then continue in stockinette st with main color. Inc 2 sts at the center (after the 1st st and before the last st of the rnd), every 8th rnd 4 (4) (4) (4) (7) times: 50 (50) (56) (56) (62) sts. When the sleeve measures 45 (46) (48) (50) (51) cm/17¾ (18) (19) (19¾) (20) in, place the center 8 (8) (10) (10) (10) underarm sts on a string. Knit the second sleeve in the same way.

Yoke: Put the sleeves and body sts on the longer cn 6 mm/US 9. There should now be 198 (204) (216) (222) (240) sts on the needle. Knit 1 rnd in color 1, then knit pattern II, following the diagram.

Neck: When you have finished knitting the pattern, continue with color 1 but change to dpn 4.5 mm/US 7 and dec to 52 (54) (56) (58) (60) sts evenly spaced around. Work 18 rnds in k1, p1 ribbing. Bind off loosely, turn the edge under, and sew it down.

Bind off the underarm sts together using an extra needle. Knit 1 st from the body with 1 st from the sleeve, then bind off as usual.

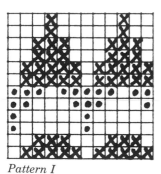

Pattern II

Pattern I

knit 2 together

main color
color 1
color 2
Skip the black squares when
these sts have been eliminated.

Boy's Cardigan— Setesdal Pattern

Photo page 50
Instructions from Rauma
Size: about 12 years
Measurements: chest: 96 cm/38 in; length: 52 cm/20½ in; sleeve width (widest point): 40 cm/15¾ in; sleeve length: 47 cm/18½ in

Yarn: 3-ply wool yarn at about 1000 yd/lb, 250 g/9 oz blue, about 150 g/6 oz white

Needles: Cn 80 cm, 2.5 mm and 3 mm/32 in, US 2 and 3; dpn 2.5 mm and 3 mm/US 2 and 3

Gauge: 23 sts = 10 cm/4 in
The cardigan is knitted in the round and cut open afterward. The sleeves are knitted starting at the top and sewn in.

Body: Using blue yarn and cn 2.5 mm/US 2, cast on 170 sts and work 9 cm/3½ in in k1, p1 ribbing. Change to cn 3 mm/US 3 and stockinette st. On the 1st rnd inc evenly spaced to 220 sts. Knit pattern I following the diagram and then knit 19 rnds in lice pattern for the background (see diagram). Knit pattern II. The body is now finished and should measure about 52 cm/20½ in.

Mark armholes; there should be 110 sts for the back and 55 sts for each half of the front (4 sts will be used in cutting the opening). Machine stitch 2 rows on each side of the center st of the front and then cut open between the rows (see page 81). Count 33 sts for the shoulder and bind them off either separately or together.

Mark the front neck opening, centering it. Machine stitch around it. Cut away the excess fabric. Set aside the 34 sts of the back neck on a string.

Front Edge: With blue yarn and dpn 2.5 mm/US 2, cast on 14 sts. Work the first 10 sts in k1, p1 ribbing and the other 4 sts in stockinette. Bind off when the piece measures about 45 cm/17¾ in. Knit the other front edge in the same way, beginning with 4 sts in stockinette, then 10 sts in ribbing. Make 9 buttonholes evenly spaced on this band (see photo page 50), one buttonhole on stitch 3 of the ribbing and another on stitch 8 of the ribbing so that the two buttonholes line

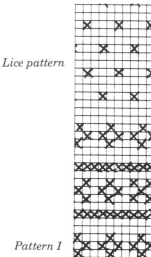

Lice pattern

Pattern I

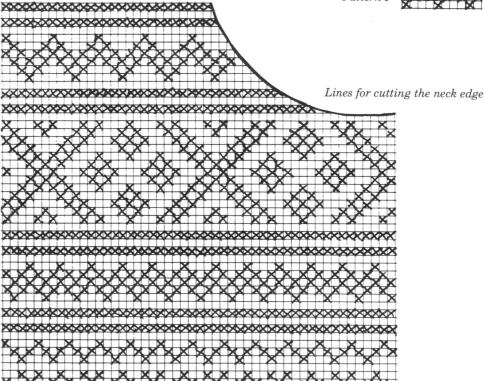

Lines for cutting the neck edge

Pattern II

up when the band is folded.

Baste the front edgings so that the cardigan's right side lies against the edging's wrong side (buttonholes on the left side). Machine stitch, keeping the seam just between the stockinette and ribbed sections. Turn the stockinette to the sweater's wrong side so that it covers the cut edges. Sew down by hand. Stitch around each buttonhole to attach the two layers of the band.

Neck: Pick up 86 sts around the neck opening with the beginning and ending centered on the button and buttonhole rows: 5 sts from the front band,

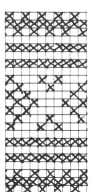

Pattern IV

21 sts around the front machine stitching, 34 sts from the string at the back, 21 sts on the other front section and 5 sts on the other band. Knit 3 rows with blue, then knit the neck portion of pattern III, and then knit 4 more rows in blue—this is the top of the neck edge. Using blue, knit as many rows as necessary to line the neck edging and cover the cut edges. Bind off. Matching right side to right side, sew the front edge seams by hand. Sew down the lining by hand. Make a button loop on the left side of the neck. Sew on 10 buttons (9 on the front edge and 1 on the neck).

Sleeves: Cast on 92 sts on dpn 3 mm/US 3 and knit 5 rnds stockinette with blue yarn. Next, begin the pattern and dec 2 sts every 10th rnd as follows: dec 1 st at the beginning of the 1st needle and dec 1 st 1 st before the end of the 4th needle. Knit pattern III from A-B, then 19 rnds lice pattern, then pattern IV. On the last pattern rnd, dec about every 4th st until 50 sts remain. Change to dpn 2.5 mm/US 2 and work 8 cm/3 in in k1, p1 ribbing. Bind off. Sew in the sleeves and cover the cut edges on the wrong side with the first blue rnds.

Sweater with Selbu Patterns

Photo page 52
Instructions from Rauma
Size: Man's
Yarn: 3-ply wool yarn at about 1000 yd/lb, 500 g/18 oz dark and 400 g/14 oz light
Needles: Cn 2 mm and 2.5 mm/US 0 and 2; dpn 2 mm and 2.5 mm/US 0 and 2
Gauge: 24 sts = 10 cm/4 in
The sweater is knitted in the round and divided at the armholes. The original model was cut up the front as a cardigan, buttoned with clasps, and had no neck edging other than binding off. We have decided not to do this but describe both alternatives.
Body: With cn 2 mm/US 0, cast on 260 sts and rib k2, p2 for 8 cm/3 in. Knit 1 rnd in stockinette with light yarn and inc to 288 sts evenly spaced around, changing to cn 2.5 mm/US 2. Knit the 32 striped rnds of the lower edge pattern following the diagram and begin the body patterns. Start with pattern III (side), pattern II (side front), pattern I (center front), pattern II (side front), pattern III (side), pattern II (side back), pattern IV (center back), pattern II (side back). If you want to cut the front open for a cardigan,

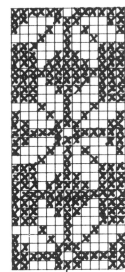

Pattern III

Side

begin in the center with pattern I, then follow the order of the other patterns. Knit in pattern for 70 rnds.

Now divide the work as follows: Knit to pattern III on one side, bind off 15 sts for the armhole, knit across the back to pattern III on the other side, and bind off 15 sts. Now there are 133 sts on the front and 125 sts on the back.
Front: Bind off 1 st on each side 4x. Knit 35 rows counted

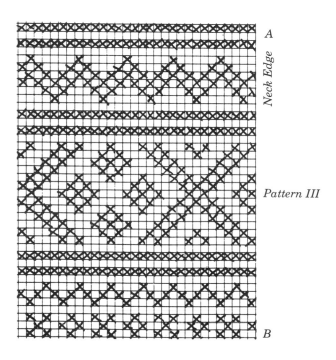

Neck Edge

Pattern III

A

B

Center Back

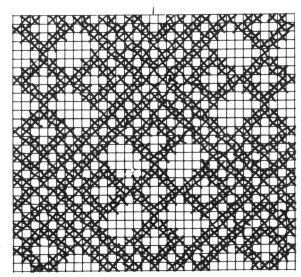

Pattern IV

Pattern II   Center   Pattern I

Center of the sleeve

Pattern for lower edge

Lower sleeve

from the binding off for the armhole. Bind off or set aside on a string the center 41 sts (pattern I). Knit the shoulder sts for 30 rows following the diagram and put those sts on a string.

Back: Bind off the armhole sts as for the front. Knit the back until it is the same length as the front. Bind off the center 33 sts or put them on a string. Bind off the back shoulder sts with the front shoulder sts.

Sleeves: Cast on 62 sts on dpn 2.5 mm/US 2 and rib k2, p2 for 7 cm/2¾ in. Then knit 19 rnds of the pattern, following the diagram. On the next rnd, inc 8 sts evenly spaced around. Knit the next 4 rnds of the pattern and then inc 8 sts evenly spaced around. Begin the sleeve pattern. A star pattern is placed on each side of the center pattern. Inc 2 sts every 6th rnd until there are 120 sts on the needle. Work the incs in patterns, first using the narrower pattern on each side of the center, then the broader pattern. Knit until there are 6 star patterns on the sleeve.

Now knit back and forth. Bind off 8 sts at the beginning of the 1st right-side row and 8 sts at the beginning of the next wrong-side row. Continue binding off 3 sts at the beginning of each row until the 7th star is finished. Bind off all sts.

Fit in and sew the sleeves. If you want a pullover, pick up the neck sts along the sides of the neck and put them with the saved sts on dpn 2 mm/US 0 and rib k2, p2 for 6 cm/2½ in. Turn the neck edge under and sew it down.

If you want to cut open the front for a cardigan, knit a border for each front edge: do 2 rows on the border for every 3 rows of the body. Sew on the borders, turn them to the inside and sew them down on the wrong side. Sew on pewter clasps.

Korsnäs Sweater

Photo page 79
Instructions written by Gretel Dahlberg
Size: 40
Yarn: 3-ply fingering weight superwash wool yarn, 300 g/11 oz natural white, 450 g/16 oz red, 300 g/11 oz green, 100 g/4 oz yellow, 50 g/2 oz light red
Needles: Cns 80 and 40 cm, 2 mm or 2.5 mm/32 and 16 in, US 0 or 2; crochet hook 2 mm or 2.5 mm
Gauge: knitting—32 sts and 40 rows = 10 cm/4 in
single crochet—32 sts and 25 rows = 10 cm/4 in
Stitch count: Body, lower edge—350 sts.
Upper sleeve—160–170 sts
Neck opening—32 sts

The crocheting is worked in the back loops of the sts of the previous rows. When changing yarn to another color, draw the strand of the new color through both sts which are on the crochet hook. All the threads used in the same row are caught with each st. The sweater begins with single crochet in the round, starting at the lower edge. The knitting is done in the round in stockinette. You

Step I

Step II

Changing to a new color

can inc the width of the sweater after 10 cm/4 in of the knitted section by increasing 1 st at each side every 10th rnd up to the armhole.

The armhole can be cut open or crocheted back and forth, with the back worked separately after the division for the armhole. Every row in crochet is worked from right to left. Cut the yarn at the end of each row and fasten it at the beginning of the next row.

The neck opening is large enough that it doesn't need to be buttoned. The sweater is crocheted together at the shoulders, or the shoulder seams can be sewn with red yarn. The

seams should be invisible.

The sleeves are crocheted separately, starting at the top. To work the crocheted section at the top of the sleeve: after the 1st 2 rnds with 160 sts, dec 2 sts every rnd 6x, then dec 2 sts every 3rd rnd 4x: center decs at the underarm. Knitted section: dec 2 sts every 6th rnd at the center of the underarm. Crocheted lower section: Dec 2 sts every 4th rnd at the center of the underarm. The decs can also be made between each pattern so that the designs will be worked evenly around. Finish the sleeve with 2 red rnds.

Turn the work and crochet the sleeve edging. Crochet 1

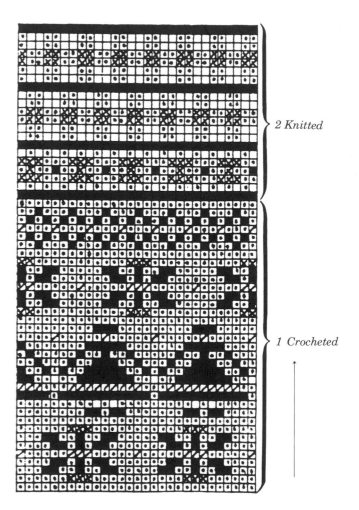

2 Knitted

1 Crocheted

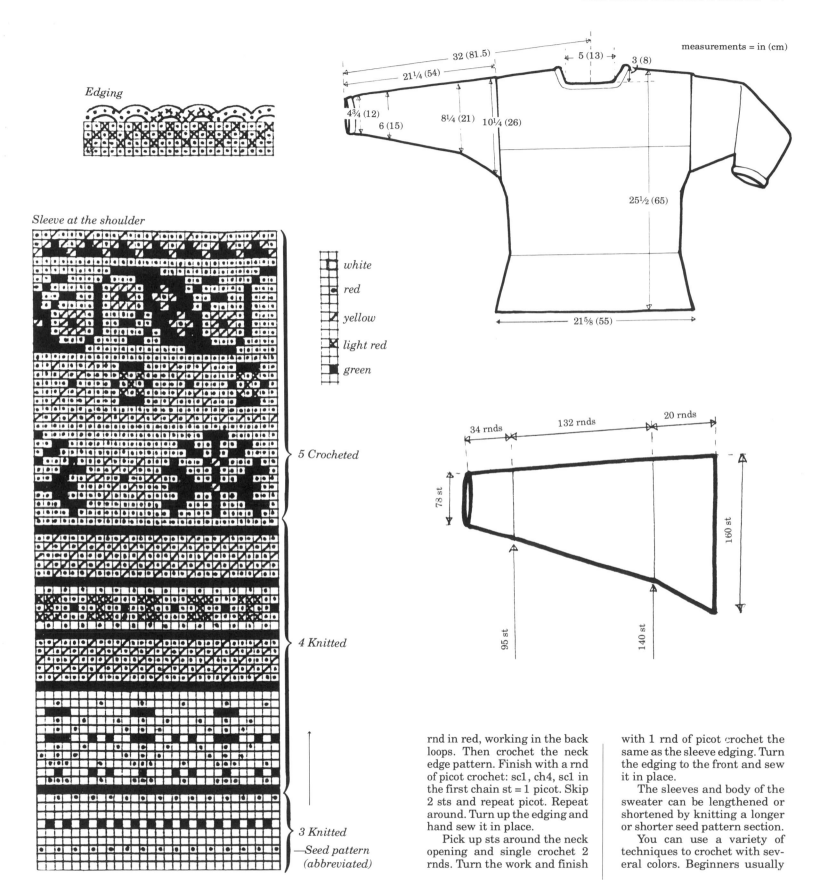

Edging

Sleeve at the shoulder

	white
	red
	yellow
	light red
	green

5 Crocheted

4 Knitted

3 Knitted

—Seed pattern
(abbreviated)

measurements = in (cm)

32 (81.5)

21¼ (54)

5 (13)

3 (8)

4¾ (12)

6 (15)

8¼ (21)

10¼ (26)

25½ (65)

21⅝ (55)

34 rnds

132 rnds

20 rnds

78 st

160 st

95 st

140 st

rnd in red, working in the back loops. Then crochet the neck edge pattern. Finish with a rnd of picot crochet: sc1, ch4, sc1 in the first chain st = 1 picot. Skip 2 sts and repeat picot. Repeat around. Turn up the edging and hand sew it in place.

Pick up sts around the neck opening and single crochet 2 rnds. Turn the work and finish with 1 rnd of picot crochet the same as the sleeve edging. Turn the edging to the front and sew it in place.

The sleeves and body of the sweater can be lengthened or shortened by knitting a longer or shorter seed pattern section.

You can use a variety of techniques to crochet with several colors. Beginners usually

Upper sleeve

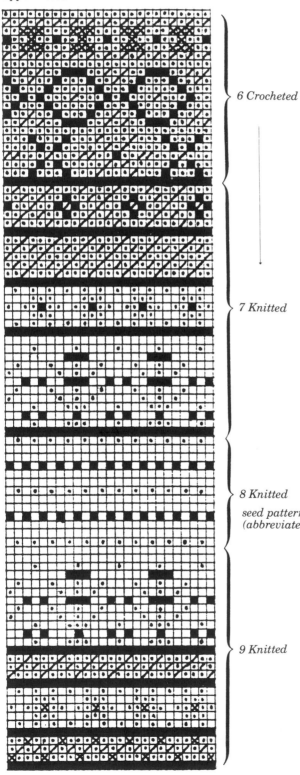

6 Crocheted

7 Knitted

8 Knitted
*seed pattern
(abbreviated)*

9 Knitted

change the yarn on the index finger every time they change to a new color in pattern crocheting. Some people also hold two different colored strands on one finger. The technique which I learned as a child was to hold only the background color strand on the index finger (red in this case) and hold the other colors of yarn in the palm. Pick up the color you need with the crochet hook in front of and behind the red thread, which lies unused on the index finger until needed again. In this way, you don't waste any time in changing yarns. This was the technique that the traditional knitters used, and they were able to make a sweater in three weeks.

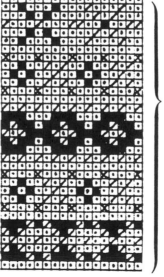

10 Crocheted

Lower sleeve

Fana Cardigan
*Photo page 43
Instructions from Rauma*

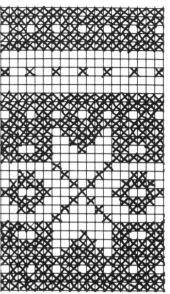

Pattern II

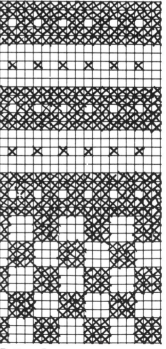

Pattern I

YARN: 3-ply wool yarn at about 1000 yd/lb

SIZE:	4 yrs	6 yrs	8 yrs	10 yrs	36	38	40/42	44	50	52
YARN AMOUNTS:										
white	6	7	9	9	9	9	11	11	13	14 oz
	150	200	250	250	250	250	300	300	350	400 g
black	7	9	11	11	11	11	13	13	14	16 oz
	200	250	300	300	300	300	350	350	400	450 g
MEASUREMENTS:										
Chest width	28	29	32	34	36	38	40	42	44	47 in
	70	75	81	86	92	97	102	108	113	119 cm
Total length	16½	19	20	21	22	23	24	25½	27	27½ in
	42	48	50	54	56	58	62	65	68	70 cm
Sleeve length	12½	14	15	16½	18	19	20	20½	22	23 in
	32	35	39	42	46	48	51	52	55	58 cm

NEEDLES: Cns 80 and 40 cm, 2.5 mm and 3 mm/32 and 16 in, US 2 and 3; dpn 2.5 mm and 3 mm/US 2 and 3

GAUGE: 24 sts = 10 cm/4 in

SLEEVES:

	4 yrs	6 yrs	8 yrs	10 yrs	36	38	40/42	44	50	52
With black yarn and dpn 2.5 mm/US 2, cast on	38	40	42	44	46	48	48	52	58	60 sts
Rib k1, p1 for about:	¾	¾	¾	1	1	1	1	1½	1½	1½ in
	2	2	2	3	3	3	3	4	4	4 cm
Change to cn 3 mm/US 3 and stockinette. Inc to	50	52	56	58	58	58	60	64	72	74 sts
Knit pattern I and then the stripes. Inc 2 sts at the underarm every	7	7	7	6	6	6	6	7	7	7 rnds
until there are	68	74	80	86	98	100	102	108	114	116 sts
on the needle. Then inc 2 sts every other rnd until there are	76	82	88	94	106	108	110	116	122	124 sts
When the sleeve measures about	9	10	12	13	14½	15	16	17	18	19 in
	23	26	30	33	37	39	41	43	46	49 cm
knit pattern II. The sleeve now measures	12½	14	15	16½	18	19	20	20½	22	23 in
	32	35	39	42	46	48	51	52	55	58 cm

Turn the sleeve inside out and knit 5 rnds in stockinette (this will cover the cut edges later). On the 2nd and 4th rnds, inc 2 sts centered at the underarm so that the edging won't be too tight. Bind off loosely.

BODY:

	4 yrs	6 yrs	8 yrs	10 yrs	36	38	40/42	44	50	52
With black yarn and cn 2.5 mm/US 2, cast on	165	177	189	201	211	221	235	251	261	271 sts
Rib k1, p1, working back and forth, for about	¾	¾	¾	¾	1	1	1	1½	1½	1½ in
	2	2	2	2	3	3	3	4	4	4 cm

Set aside 11 sts on each side on a string for the front edges and knit the rest of the sts in the round.

	4 yrs	6 yrs	8 yrs	10 yrs	36	38	40/42	44	50	52
Change to cn 3 mm and stockinette, increasing to	169	181	193	205	217	229	247	259	271	283 sts

Then knit pattern I. The 4 sts at the center front should be knitted with only one color (they'll be used for the front edge seams).

	4 yrs	6 yrs	8 yrs	10 yrs	36	38	40/42	44	50	52
When the pattern stripes are begun, the st count should be	173	186	199	212	225	238	251	264	277	290 sts
Knit the stripe rows until the body measures about	12½	14	15	16½	18	19	19½	20½	22½	23 in
	32	35	39	42	46	48	50	52	55	58 cm

Then knit the star pattern, followed by 2 stripes. The sweater can be lengthened by knitting more stripe rows. Finish with 1 rnd in a color different from that used in the last stripe row.

	4 yrs	6 yrs	8 yrs	10 yrs	36	38	40/42	44	50	52
The body now measures about	16½	19	19½	21	22	23	24	25½	27	27½ in
	42	48	50	54	56	58	62	65	68	70 cm

ASSEMBLY:

Weave in all loose threads and press the pieces lightly. Machine stitch a double row in the center front and along the armhole (see page 81). Machine stitch around the neck opening, about 1/3 of half the body width and about

	4 yrs	6 yrs	8 yrs	10 yrs	36	38	40/42	44	50	52
	¾	¾	¾	¾	1	1	1	1½	1½	1½ in
	2	2	2	2	3	3	3	4	4	4 cm

Set aside 11 sts on each side on a string for the front edges and knit the rest of the sts in the round.

	4 yrs	6 yrs	8 yrs	10 yrs	36	38	40/42	44	50	52
Change to cn 3 mm and stockinette, increasing to	169	181	193	205	217	229	247	259	271	283 sts
Then knit pattern I. The 4 sts at the center front should be	1	1	1½	1½	1½	1½	2	2	2	2 in
	3	3	4	4	4	4	5	5	5	5 cm

deep at the center. Bind off the shoulder sts from the back side and cut away any excess fabric at the neck opening.

FRONT EDGES:

Put the edge sts on dpn 2.5 mm/US 2 and cast on 4 more sts at the inside (for the seam). Work the edging in k1, p1 ribbing and the seam section in stockinette.

	4 yrs	6 yrs	8 yrs	10 yrs	36	38	40/42	44	50	52
Knit until the edging is about	⅜	⅜	¾	¾	¾	¾	¾	¾	¾	¾ in
	1	1	2	2	2	2	2	2	2	2 cm

shorter than the measurement of the body up to the neck opening. Bind off the 4 seam sts and put the rest of the sts on a string. Don't forget to make buttonholes in one edge. Knit the button edging first, then mark it for placement of the number of buttons you want. Make buttonholes to correspond on the opposite edge.

NECK EDGE:

	4 yrs	6 yrs	8 yrs	10 yrs	36	38	40/42	44	50	52
Pick up about	86	88	90	92	100	100	104	104	108	108 sts

on dpn or short cn 2.5 mm/US 2. The front edging sts are part of these st counts.

	4 yrs	6 yrs	8 yrs	10 yrs	36	38	40/42	44	50	52
Work in k1, p1 ribbing for about	2	2	2	2	2	2	2	2½	2½	2⅜ in
	5	5	5	5	5	5	5	6	6	6 cm

Bind off loosely, turn the edges under, and sew them down so that the cut edges are covered.

Ljusdal Cardigan

Photo page 67
Instructions written by Inger Rosell

Size: 36 (40) (42/44)
Actual Measurements: 90 (100) (110) cm/35½ (39½) (43¼) in
Length: 45 (50) (55) cm/17¾ (19¾) (21¾) in
Yarn: 2-ply wool yarn at about 1450 yd/lb, 400 g/14 oz red, 200 g/7 oz white, 200 g/7 oz green

Needles: Cns 80 and 40 cm, 2 mm or 2.5 mm/32 and 16 in, US 0 or 2; dpn 2 mm or 2.5 mm/US 0 or 2
Gauge: 30 sts = 10 cm/4 in
Body: Cast on 300 (315) (330) sts on the longer cn. Knit 1 rnd with red yarn, purl 1 rnd with white. Repeat 6x. Then knit 5 rnds in stockinette with red. Work pattern III in white, 10 rnds red, pattern III with green, 10 rnds red.

Now knit pattern 1B and, at the same time, start the zigzag pattern at the sides. When the piece measures 22 (27) (32) cm/8½ (10½) (12½) in, knit in the date and initials at the center front. After the initials, work 5 rnds with red. Bind off the center 50 (55) (55) sts above the monogram.

Then, knit back and forth on the cn until the piece measures about 37 (42) (47) cm/14½ (16½) (18½) in. Knit the shoulder pattern following the diagram. At 43 (48) (53) cm/17 (19) (21) in, bind off 35 (40) (45) sts at the center back. Knit the other shoulder to match. Bind off.

Sleeves: Using dpn, cast on 60 (60) (70) sts and knit 1 rnd red. Purl 1 rnd white, knit 1 rnd red 3x, and then knit pattern 1A. On the next rnd, inc to 90 sts, evenly spaced around. Knit 12 rnds red and then pattern 1B, working side pattern II at the inner fold line where a seam would be. For size 36, knit 3 white and 3 green patterns; for sizes 40 and 42/44, knit 4 white and 3 green patterns. After each pattern, inc evenly on the next rnd as follows:

after the 1st white pattern 8 sts: 98 sts

after the 1st green pattern 12 sts: 110 sts

after the second white pattern 11 sts: 121 sts

after the second green pattern 15 sts: 136 sts

after the third white pattern 10 sts: 146 sts

For size 36, the incs stop when pattern 1B is knitted. For sizes 40 and 42/44, inc 8 sts after the third green pattern (154 sts).

Do not inc after the 4th white pattern but before pattern III, inc 1 st at each side of the side pattern. Knit the upper arm pattern following the diagram. Finish with 5 rnds red. Put the 27 sts at the center of the underarm on a string and bind off the remaining sts. On the 27 reserved sts, knit an underarm gusset following the diagram.

Assembly: Mark the location of the sleeves on the body; machine stitch and cut open (see page 81). Sew in the sleeves. Mark the center front. Stitch and cut open.

Use a narrow woven band to line the front edges, neck opening, and wrong side of the armholes. Sew the band with edges meeting on the neck opening and front edges. Turn the band under and sew it down. At the armholes, lay the band over the seams and sew it down. Sew hooks and eyes to the wrong side of the front edges.

Zigzag pattern for the side   *Pattern 1B*

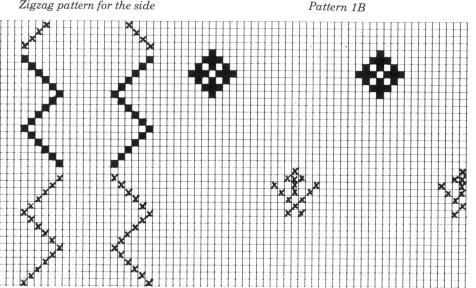

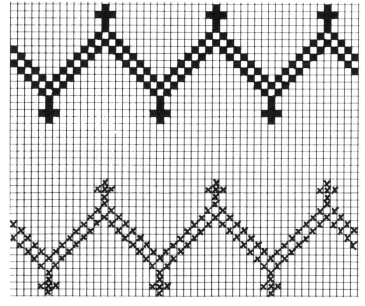

Pattern III

Upper sleeve

Monogram

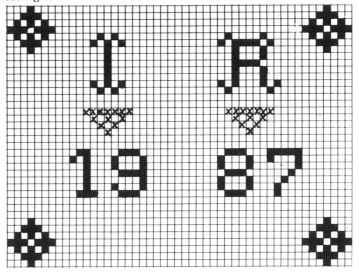

Shoulder section

Placement of patterns

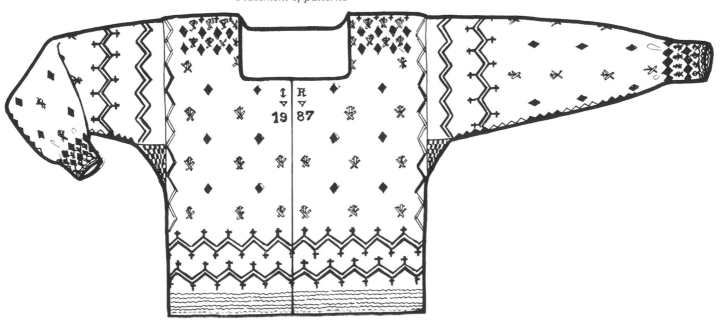

Ljusdal cardigan

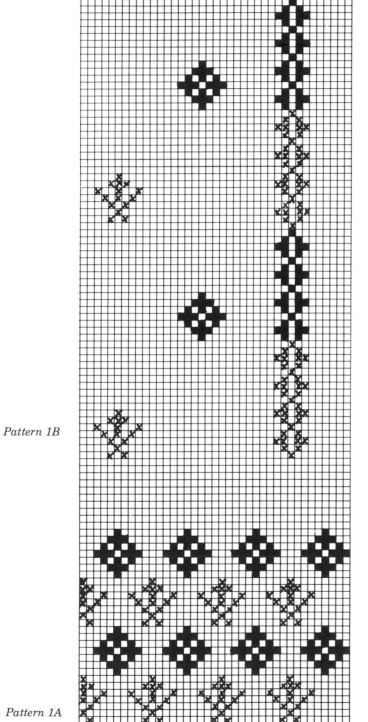

Pattern 1B

Pattern 1A

Lower sleeve

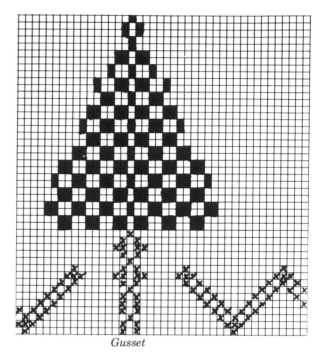

Gusset

Upper sleeve

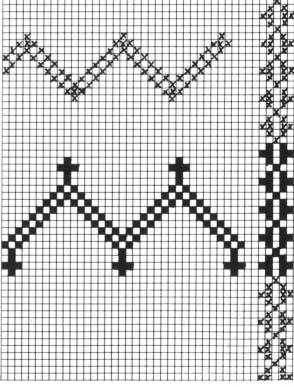

Side pattern II

Jacket with Knitted Sleeves

Photo page 64
Design and Instructions by Anne Deval and Mette Olsen. Pattern for the sleeves is from the Dalarna Museum.

Size: XS/12 years (S/34–36) (M/38–40) (L/42); child/4-6 years

Width—women's sizes: 86 (90) (97) (103) cm/33¾ (35½) (38) (40½) in

Width—child's size: 65 cm/ 25½ in

Length—women's sizes: 55 (59) (61) (64) cm/21½ (23¼) (24) (25¼) in

Length—child's size: 37 cm/ 14½ in

The jacket has sleeves knitted in the round which are sewn onto a lined cloth body.

Sewing Instructions: Begin by drawing the pattern to full scale on paper and cut it out. The neck facing follows the same lines as the back piece.

On the front edge, mark the placement of 5 buttonholes. The top one should be about 1.5 cm/½ in down from the neck edge, and the lowest one should be about 5 cm/2 in from the lower edge.

Lay out the pattern pieces on the fabric. Add the following amounts for seam allowances: 5 cm/2 in at the lower edge, 2 cm/¾ in at the shoulders and sides, 1 cm/¼ in for the rest of the seams. Mark the buttonholes. Cut out the front and back pieces and the back facing.

Sew the shoulder and side seams. Sew the shoulder seams of the facing. Right sides together, sew the facing to the neck and lower edges of the front.

Cut the lining in the same way as the jacket, except at the center front, where you should follow the dotted line. Sew the shoulder and side seams of the lining. Press the seams open and sew the lining into the jacket. Baste the lining and jacket together at the armholes, zigzagging the edges. Baste in the knitted sleeves with a 1-cm/¼-in seam allowance, adjusting the extra width

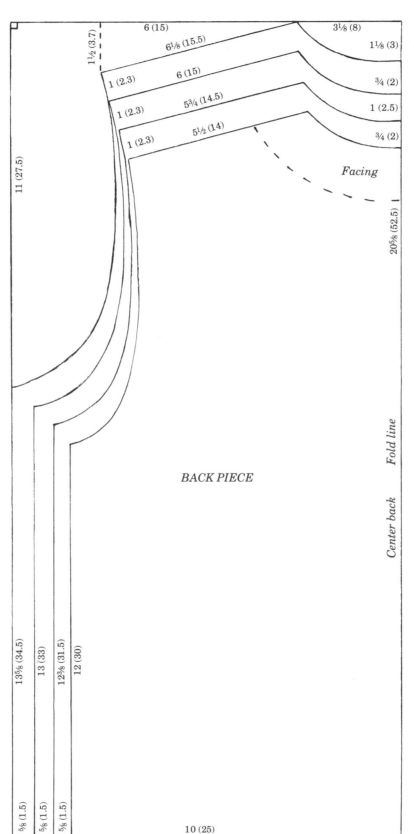

Jacket body—women's sizes

Facing

BACK PIECE

Center back / *Fold line*

measurements = in (cm)

Jacket body—women's sizes

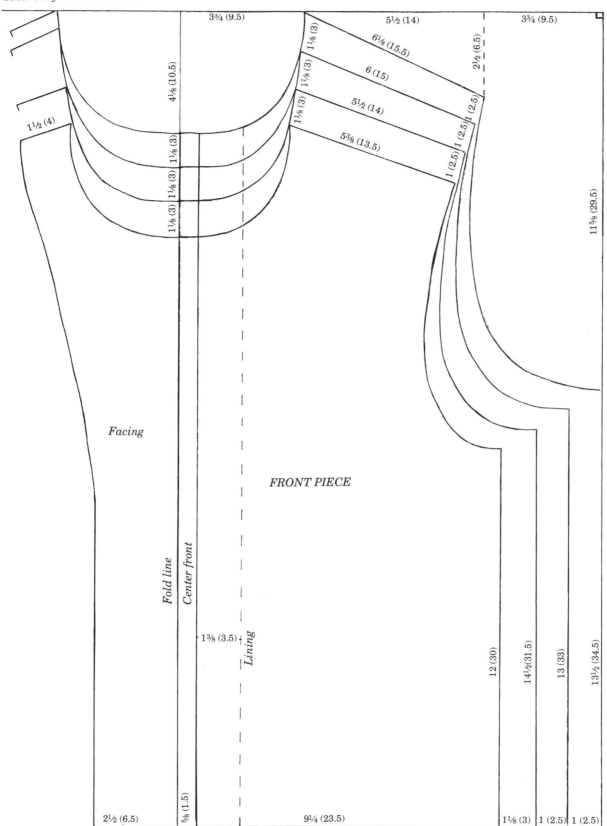

3¾ (9.5)

5½ (14)

3¾ (9.5)

6⅛ (15.5)

1⅛ (3)

6 (15)

1⅛ (3)

2½ (6.5)

5½ (14)

1⅛ (3)

4⅛ (10.5)

5⅜ (13.5)

1 (2.5)

1 (2.5)

1½ (4)

1 (2.5)

11⅝ (29.5)

1⅛ (3)

1⅛ (3)

1⅛ (3)

Facing

Fold line

Center front

FRONT PIECE

Lining

1⅜ (3.5)

12 (30)

14½ (31.5)

13 (33)

13½ (34.5)

2½ (6.5)

⅝ (1.5)

9¼ (23.5)

1⅛ (3)

1 (2.5)

1 (2.5)

measurements = in (cm)

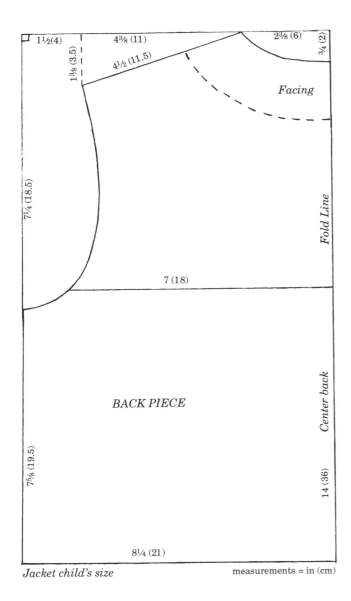

1½(4) 4⅜ (11) 2⅜ (6)

¾ (2)

1⅜ (3.5)

4½ (11.5)

Facing

7¼ (18.5)

7 (18)

Fold Line

Center back

BACK PIECE

7⅝ (19.5)

14 (36)

8¼ (21)

Jacket child's size   measurements = in (cm)

VI

V

IV

III

II

I

at the shoulders. Sew in the sleeves.

Knitted Sleeves—child 4 to 6 years
Yarn: 2- or 3-ply fingering weight wool yarn, 100 g/4 oz each black and red
Needles: dpn 2.5 mm/US 2
Gauge: 36 sts and 39 rows = 10 cm/4 in

With two strands of red yarn, cast on 54 sts and knit the first 20 rnds, changing threads and twisting the yarn after 2 sts. On the next rnd change to a single strand and inc 34 sts evenly spaced around. Knit 2 rnds in red and then begin with pattern diagram I; knit it twice with 3 red rnds in between.

On the following rnd, inc 28 sts: 116 sts. Knit 5 rnds in red. Then knit the star pattern, following diagram II–VI with 6 single-color rnds between each pattern.

Sleeve shaping—right arm:
At the same time as the 6th star is begun, begin binding off for the arm shaping. The sleeve should measure about 31 cm/12¼ in. Bind off 5 sts and work across the row. Turn and bind off 3 sts on the wrong side. Then bind off at the beginning of every knit row as follows:

5 sts 1x, 2 sts 4x, 1 st 10x, 3 sts 4x, 6 sts 2x. At the same time, bind off at the beginning of the purl rows: 3 sts 1x, 2 sts 16 x, 3 sts 2x, 5 sts 2x. Then bind off all remaining sts.

Knit the left sleeve, reversing the shaping.

Work in the loose threads, press, and sew the sleeves into the jacket armholes.

Knitted Sleeves—women's sizes

Size: XS/12 years (S) (M) (L)

Yarn: 150 g/6 oz each black and green

Needles and gauge: as above

Using black yarn, cast on 72 sts on dpn and knit 1 rnd with two strands. Change threads and twist the yarns after 2 sts. Then switch to single strands of two colors and begin the check pattern following diagram I, which is 24 rnds.

Now inc 48 sts on a black rnd and then knit following diagram II for 7 rnds. Inc another 48 sts on a black rnd: 168 sts. Knit the pattern on diagram III. Repeat the flower pattern (24 rnds) 5x and then begin binding off for the sleeve shaping for size SX. For sizes S and M, knit another 8 rnds and for size L, knit 16 rnds.

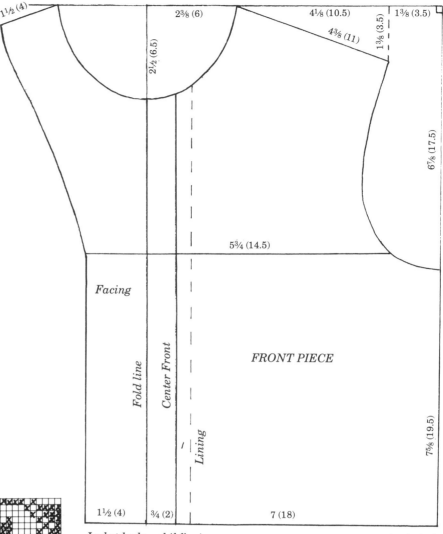

Jacket body—child's size   measurements = in (cm)

III

II

I

Sleeve Shaping—right arm:

Bind off 12 (12) (18) (8) sts and work across the row. Turn and bind off 8 (8) (6) (4) sts. At the beginning of every knit row, bind off 12 (12) (10) (8) sts 1x, 3 sts 4x (4x) (4x) (4x), 1 st 15x (15x) (17x) (22x), 2 sts 5x (5x) (5x) (2x), 5 sts 5x (5x) (5x) (5x). At the same time, at the beginning of every purl row, bind off 8 (8) (6) (4) sts 1x, 4 (4) (4) (4) sts 4x, 2 sts 8x (8x) (10x) (10x), 1 st 7x (7x) (7x) (7x), 2 sts 5x (5x) (5x) (7x), 5 sts 3x (3x) (3x) (3x). Bind off all remaining sts.

Knit the left sleeve, reversing the shaping. Press the sleeve it and sew it into the jacket.

Night Sweater

Photo page 23
Instructions written by
Kristina Lindkvist
Size: 36 (40) (44)
Width: 92 (104) (112) cm/36¼ (41) (44) in
Yarn: 2- or 3-ply fingering weight wool yarn, 600 g/21 oz
Needles: Cn 80 cm, 2.5 mm/32 in, US 2; spn 2.5 mm/US 2; dpn 2.5 mm/US 2
Gauge: 24 sts and 34 rows = 10 cm/4 in

The lower edge is knitted on straight needles; the body is knitted in the round. The armholes are cut open afterward. The sleeves are knitted in the round, beginning at the cuffs.

Lower Edge: With spn 2.5 mm/US 2, cast on 111 (125) (135) sts and work k2, p2 ribbing for 5 cm/2 in, shifting the sts as indicated on the diagram. Cut the yarn. Cast on the same number of sts and knit the other lower edge.

Body: Put all of the sts of the lower edges—222 (250) (270) sts—on a cn and knit the pattern with purl sts on a stockinette background, following the diagram up to the neck opening at the center front. Lengthen or shorten the length (58 cm/22¾ in) if you wish by adding or eliminating a complete pattern. Bind off the center front sts and continue working each side of the body on spn. For the front neck opening on all sizes, bind off 16, 2, 1 sts on each side following the diagram. Finish knitting the shoulders and bind off 35 sts for the back neck opening, then 2 sts at each side following the diagram.

Sleeves: Cast on 51 (53) (57) sts evenly divided on four dpn and knit, following the diagram. Inc 1 st at each side of the sleeve underarm (2 sts every 8th rnd and every 6th rnd) following the diagram. The rnds begin with the 2 sts of the side stripe pattern, alternating 2 knit sts for 2 rnds and 2 purl sts for 2 rnds. Make sure that these 2 sts stay on the same needle. Follow the diagram and bind off all sts at desired arm length. Knit the other sleeve in the

Details of side stripe pattern
V = inc 1 st
× = purl st

same way.

Sew the shoulder seams; cut the armhole and sew in the sleeves (see page 81).

Neck: With the cn, pick up about 120 sts around the neck opening from the right side with the cn. Knit 4 rows back and forth. On the 2nd row, dec 2 sts evenly spaced on the back side; on the front side 1 st in each corner over the neck edges 2, 1. Bind off.

Triangular Shawl

Photo page 48
Instructions from the Norwegian Handicraft Union, adapted from a shawl in the Norwegian Folk Museum's collections.

Yarn: 2-ply wool yarn at about 1750 yd/lb, about 300 g/11 oz

Needles: 2 cns 80 cm, 3.5 mm/32 in, US 5; crochet hook 3 mm

Cast on 580 sts. Mark the center with a contrasting thread. Knit back and forth for 16 rows in garter st. Begin the decs on the 2nd row: bind off 2 sts at the beginning of the row, knit until 2 sts before the center, ssk, k2 tog on the 2 sts after the center marking, then end the row with k2 tog. On the 3rd row, bind off 2 sts at the beginning of the row, do not increase at center, k2 tog at the end of the row. Alternate these two dec rows throughout the shawl.

After the 16th garter-st row, begin the lace pattern over 23 rows:

Row 1: (260 sts to the center) Bind off 2 sts, *k2 tog, yo*, repeat *–* 127 times, k1 (center: 259 sts remain), k1, *yo, k2 tog*, repeat *–*. End row with k2 tog.

Rows 2–4: garter st, continuing to alternate dec rows.

Row 5: lace pattern as in row 1.

Rows 6–8: garter st, continuing to alternate dec rows.

Rows 9–15: Work k1, p1 rib for 7 rows, continuing to alternate dec rows.

Rows 16–18: garter st, continuing to alternate dec rows.

Row 19: lace pattern: bind off 2

sts, k1, *k2 tog, yo*, repeat *–* to the center, k1, *yo, k2 tog*, repeat *–*. End row with k1, k2 tog.

Rows 20–22: garter st, continuing to alternate dec rows.

Row 23: lace pattern as in row 19.

Rows 24–40: garter st, continuing to alternate dec rows.

Repeat rows 1–40. Continue the decs at the center as before until all the sts are gone.

Edging: Crochet 2 rows around the whole shawl. Begin on the corner of the cast-on edge with ch3, *1 hdc, ch1, skip 1 st*, repeat *–*. At the center back, work 2 hdc in the same st. Continue along the bound-off edges as follows: *ch3, 1 slip st in the bound-off sts*, repeat *–*. At the corner, make 2 dc in the same st as the 1 st ch. Finish with 1 slip st in the previous row's chain st. Finish with 1 row of picot edging.

Tie 9-cm/3½-in fringes in the last crochet row along the cast-on edge.

Selbu Mitten

Photo page 53

Size: Woman's (Man's)

Yarn: 2- or 3-ply wool yarn at about 1000 yd/lb, 35 g/2 oz each light and dark

Needles: dpn 1.75 mm or 2 mm/US 00 or 0

Gauge: 17 sts and 19 rows = 5 cm/2 in

With dark yarn, cast on 64 (80) sts evenly divided on four dpn. Knit the wrist following the diagram. On the last dark-only rnd after the star pattern of the wrist, dec 4 sts evenly spaced on the rnd.

Continue following the diagram, putting the star pattern on the back of the hand and working the palm in the striped designs without the star. Inc 2 sts for the thumb every other rnd for the thumb gusset (which is knitted in check pattern) until there are 24 (28) thumb sts. Put the thumb sts on a string or stitch holder, cast on 5 sts over the thumbhole, and continue following the diagram until the mitten reaches the little finger. Dec 2 sts on each side—4 sts every rnd—until 12 sts remain. Cut yarn, draw through sts, and tie off.

Thumb: Divide the 24 (28) sts onto two needles and pick up another 9 sts for the inside of the thumb. The outside is patterned in small checks (1 × 1 st), while the inside is patterned with large checks (2 × 2 sts—see diagram B). Dec 2 sts every other row until the work reaches the top of the thumbnail. Then dec 4 sts every rnd twice. Cut yarn, draw through remaining sts, and tie off.

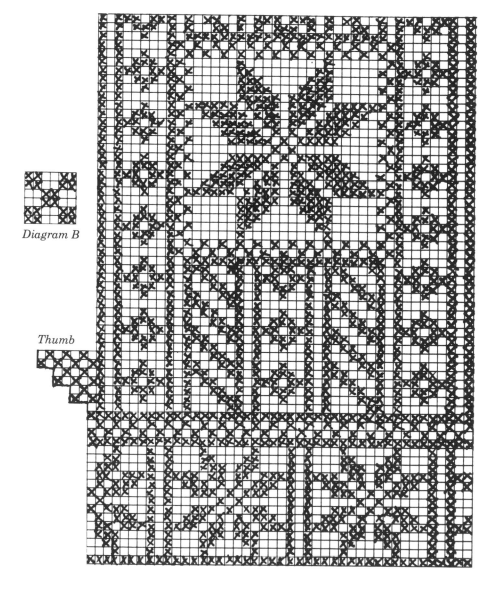

Diagram B

Thumb

Faroese Shawl

Center back

Begin here

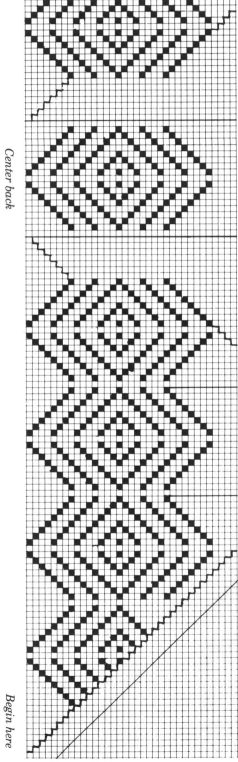

Faroese Lace Pattern Shawl

Photo page 29
Instructions from Faroese Handicrafts, translated and rewritten by Christina Westman-Janson

Size: Center back length (without fringe) about 77 cm/30¼ in
Yarn: 2-ply worsted weight wool yarn, about 400 g/14 oz
Needles: 2 cns 80 cm, 5 mm/32 in, US 7; spn 5 mm/US 7; crochet hook 4 mm (for the fringe) The shawl is knitted in garter st and a lace pattern, starting at the bottom. As the lace pattern is rather complicated, make a sample swatch to see how the yarn overs and decs affect the way patterns slant to the right or left.

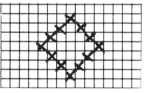

Sample swatch

Sample Swatch: Cast on 13 sts and knit 1 row. Knit all odd-numbered rows.
Row 2: k6, yo, k2 tog, k5.
Row 4 (the pattern widens diagonally): k4, k2 tog, yo, k1, yo, k2 tog, k4.
Row 6: k3, k2 tog, yo, k3, yo, k2 tog, k3.
Row 8: k2, k2 tog, yo, k5, yo, k2 tog, k2.
Row 10 (the pattern narrows diagonally): k4, yo, k2 tog, k1, k2 tog, yo, k4.
Row 12: k5, yo, ssk, yo, k5.
Row 14: k6, yo, k2 tog, k5.
Shawl: Cast on 461 sts on cn (5 edge, 216 side, 19 center gore, 216 side, 5 edge). Knit back and forth on the two cns. When the number of sts has decreased enough, change to one cn.
   Knit 2 rows and begin decs:

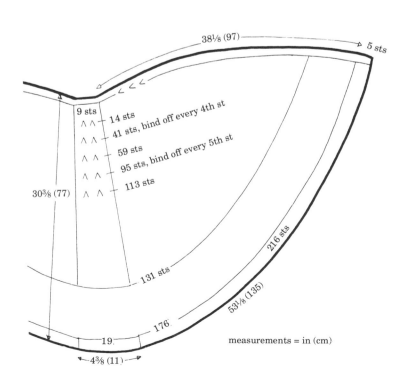

measurements = in (cm)

dec 1 st inside the 5 edge sts at each side, every other row. Likewise, dec 1 st on each side of the 19 center gore sts. Mark the dec points with a thread or plastic ring, and move the markers as you work.

After 40 rows, make a lace row: *k2 tog, yo*, repeat *–*. Knit 1 row and then knit the lace pattern following the diagram.

When the lace patterns on the sides meet the center gore, don't dec on either side of the gore (the last 34 rows). After that, continue decreasing as before (following the diagram). The decs on the shawl's outer edges continue as established.

When the lace is finished, there are 5 + 131 + 19 + 131 + 5 sts left. Continue in garter stitch.

When each side section has 113 sts, dec 1 st on each inner side of the gore. Repeat this dec until each side section has 95, 59, 41, and 14 sts left. Thus, the gore's 19 sts dec to 9 sts.

The extra decreasing for the shoulders on the side sections is done when there are 95 sts remaining: k3, k2 tog 18x on each side. Dec for the shoulders again when there are 41 sts left: k2, k2 tog 9x on each side.

When the last dec has been made, dec 2 sts on each side of the gore and 2 sts on each edge every other row until 2 sts remain on each side of the gore. Bind off the 13 sts.

Fringe: Wrap yarn around a piece of cardboard 14 cm/5½ in wide; cut the yarn at one end and use 3 threads for each fringe. Double the yarn and draw it through every other st with the crochet hook and tie with a loop. Spread the shawl out along the edge of a table and cut the fringe evenly.

Selbu Glove

Photo page 53
Instructions from Rauma
Size: Woman's
Yarn: 3-ply wool yarn at about 1000 yd/lb, 50 g/2 oz each dark and light
Needles: Dpn 2.5 mm/US 2

Cast on 48 sts with the light yarn and rib k2, p2 for 7 cm/2¾ in, adding dark stripes as shown in the diagram. Inc 3 sts on the next rnd and knit the little chain pattern. Dec 1 st in the next plain light row. Then knit the pattern beginning at the arrow. Knit the first row of the pattern for the back of the hand, with the edge st at the left side. Then begin the gusset for the thumb: 1 light st, 1 dark st, inc 1 light st in the dark. Knit 1 dark st (center), inc 1 light in it, knit 1 dark, etc. (The dots in the diagram show how the incs are made).

Knit around and work the pattern for the palm following the diagram. Continue to inc for the thumb gusset as indicated by the dots until you are 8 rows up from the beginning of the star. Inc last 2 sts for the thumb gusset, then knit the 13 thumb sts with a contrasting yarn, put these back on the left needle and knit with the pattern yarns. Knit another 15 rnds to complete the star and then divide the glove's 60 sts for the fingers: begin on the palm after the edge st. Place the sts on a string or stitch holder. Use 9 sts for the index finger, 7 sts for the middle finger, 7 sts for the ring finger, and 7 sts for the little finger. Back of the hand: little finger 7 sts (including edge st), ring finger 7 sts, middle finger 7 sts, and index finger 9 sts.

Index finger: Pick up the 18 sts from the front and back of the hand. Cast on 6 new sts between them and knit the pattern, following the diagram, with the background color on the inside as before. Knit 20 rnds and then dec 1 st on each side of the pattern stripe until 8 sts remain. Cut yarn and draw through sts.

Middle finger: Pick up the 14 sts + 6 sts at base of index finger. Cast on 6 new sts next to the ring finger. Knit 23 rnds and dec as above.

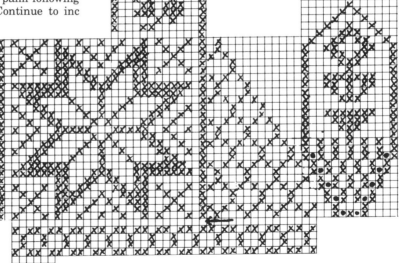

Ring finger: Pick up 14 sts + 6 at the base of the middle finger. Cast on 5 new sts at the base of the little finger. Knit 20 rnds and dec as above.

Little finger: Pick up the 14 sts + 5 sts at the base of the ring-finger. Knit 19 rnds and dec as above.

Thumb: Draw the contrasting thread out and pick up the 13 sts from the bottom of the thumbhole, 13 sts from the top of the thumbhole, and 1 st at each side. Knit the thumb following the diagram.

Mitten with a Pattern from Tjöck

Photo page 73
Size: Woman's
Yarn: 2-ply wool yarn at about 1750 yd/lb. If the main-color yarn knits to gauge, then it is all right to use yarns of slightly varying weights for the patterns.
Needles: Dpn 1.75 mm or 2 mm/US 00 or 0
Gauge: 17 sts and 18 rows = 5 cm/2 in

Cast on 64 sts with the pattern color and divide the sts evenly on four needles. Work 1 rnd of k1, p1 ribbing with a pattern color. Change to the

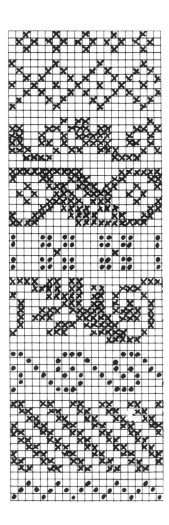

main color and continue ribbing for 3 cm/1¼ in.

Knit 1 rnd with the main color and inc 8 sts evenly spaced around. Now continue in stockinette and the patterns. Choose patterns from the diagram. If the patterns do not fit into the st count, adjust the number of sts by increasing or decreasing.

After 4 patterns, or when the whole piece measures 11–12 cm/4¼–4¾ in, put 18 sts on a string or stitch holder for the thumb. Cast on 18 sts over those put aside and continue in stockinette-st patterns.

When the mitten reaches the top of the little finger, begin the top decs. Working the decs at the two sides, one side directly above the thumb hole, dec 4 sts on every rnd. Continue decreasing until 12 sts remain. Cut yarn and draw it through the remaining sts.

Thumb: Put the thumb's 18 sts on a needle and pick up another 18 sts around the thumbhole. Knit around on 3 needles in pattern. When the thumb is halfway up the thumbnail, begin decreasing on two sides. Dec 4 sts on every rnd until 8 sts remain. Draw the yarn through the sts.

Checkerboard Mitten from Jutland

Photo page 16
Instructions from the Herning Museum
Size: Woman and child (about 10 years)
Yarn: 2-ply sport weight wool yarn, 100 g/4 oz each of two colors will make one pair for a woman or two pairs for a child.
Needles: Dpn 3 mm/US 3
Gauge: 28 sts and 30 rows = 10 cm/4 in
Woman's size: With a size 3 mm (US 3) dpn, begin by holding together one strand of each color and casting on 1 double stitch. Then divide the two strands onto finger and thumb and continue with a standard cast-on. Cast on 56 sts; the yarn which loops around the index finger (color 2) will form the sts and the yarn around the thumb (color 1) will form the edge. Divide the sts onto four needles, 14 sts on each needle.
Rnds 1 and 2: *k1 color 1, p1 color 2*, repeat *–*.
Rnd 3: change colors, knit light sts over the dark sts and vice versa, knit all the sts in the rnd.
Rnds 4 and 5: *k2 color 2, k2 color 1*, repeat *–*.
Rnds 6 and 7: change colors, knitting light sts over the dark sts and vice versa, *k2 color 1, k2 color 2*, repeat *–*.
Repeat pattern rnds 4-7. Knit 12 patterns of 2 pattern rnds each, for a total of 24 rnds. Continue the color pattern while working incs on the first and third needles. For the left mitten, work incs at the beginning of the needles; for the right mitten, work incs at their ends. Inc 1 st on first and third needles every round 4x: 64 sts.

Sample color pattern (left mitten): on the first inc round, add one st in color to match the 2 sts following. On second inc round, match new st to previous 2 sts. On third inc round, match new st to following st (a new 2-st unit). On fourth inc rnd, match new st to previous st (another new 2-st unit). The pattern continues its 2-st-by-2-

row alternation as before.

On the following rnd, put the first 10 sts (for the left mitten) on a stitch holder (the last 10 sts for the right mitten). Cast on 10 new sts on the next rnd and continue in pattern over 64 sts until the mitten reaches the tip of the little finger.

Divide the sts evenly on the needles. On the next rnd, begin the decs at the beginning of each needle: k1 and put it back on the left needle. Put the needle into the next st as if to purl and draw it over the st knitted first. Slip the knitted st back on the right needle.

Knit 1 rnd without decreasing and then dec on every rnd at the beginning of each needle until 2 sts remain on each. Draw the yarn through the remaining sts.
Thumb: Pick up 10 sts from the thumbhole plus 2 sts on each side. Pick up the 10 sts from the stitch holder and divide the 24 sts evenly on three needles. Knit 8 patterns (16 rnds) or desired length. Make the decs at the beginning of each needle until 2 sts remain on each. Draw the yarn through the remaining sts.
Child's size (10 years): Cast on 52 sts and follow the instructions above. Knit 10 patterns (20 rnds). Inc as above until there are 60 sts, setting aside 8 sts for the thumb. Continue knitting in pattern with 60 sts. Knit 9 patterns (18 rnds) or to desired length. Dec as above.
Thumb: Pick up 8 sts from the thumbhole, 2 sts at each side and the 8 sts from the stitch holder (20 sts) and divide them on three needles (7 + 7 + 6). Knit 5 patterns (10 rnds) or to desired length. Dec as above.

Man's Mitten from Varanger

Photo page 55
Instructions by Nelly Must / Sør-Varanger Museum
Yarn: sport weight wool yarn in three colors: white, red, and blue
Needles: Dpn 2.5 mm or 3 mm/US 2 or 3

Cast on 56 sts in white and divide them evenly on four needles. Rib k2, p2 for 20 rnds. Knit 1 rnd and inc 4 sts evenly: 60 sts.

Knit the pattern following the diagram. Then knit 2 rnds white and mark the place for the thumb. Knit 12 sts with contrasting yarn, put those sts back on the left needle, and knit them with the mitten yarn. Continue for 45 rnds and then begin top decs.

Thumb: Draw the contrast thread out, pick up the sts on four needles + 1 extra st on each side so that there are 7 sts on each needle. Knit 24 rnds and dec for the top.

Plait a cord about 18 cm/7 in long. Make a tassel for the end of it with all the colors from the mitten. Fasten it to the edge of the ribbing.

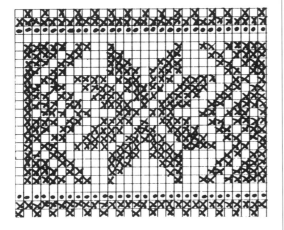

Gauntlet Mitten with Gotland Patterns

Photo page 62
The pattern is from Hermanna Stengård's collection at Gotland Handicrafts in Visby.
Size: Woman's
Yarn: 2-ply wool yarn at about 1600 yd/lb
Needles: Dpn 2 mm/US 0
The gauntlet is knitted double and has a striped lining. An interesting detail is the little ribbed border which decorates the gauntlet's lower edge.
Gauntlet: With main color, cast on 56 sts evenly divided on four needles. Knit around and inc 1 st on each needle during the first 3 rnds. Then inc 1 st every other needle, every 3rd rnd. (Be sure that the incs are evenly spaced around. For example, row 1: inc on needles 1 and 3, row 4: inc on needles 2 and 4, etc.) The gauntlet lining is striped in several colors. Continue the incs until there are 84 sts and then work even until the piece measures 9 cm/3½ in.

Knit a lace row: *k2, draw one st over the other* repeat *–* around. The gauntlet is turned at this rnd.

On the next rnd, k2 in every st so that there are 84 sts again. Knit 1 rnd. On the next rnd, inc 8 sts evenly spaced around. Choose patterns (see also page 63) and knit in pattern with two colors.

Begin decreasing after 2 cm/¾ in from the hole rnd. Dec 2 sts every 3rd rnd for 3 cm/1¼ in. Then dec 2 sts every other rnd. On the last 3 rnds on

the gauntlet, dec evenly around to 56 sts.

Turn the gauntlet at the hole rnd and pick up all the sts from the cast-on edge, and one by one, knit them together with the sts on the needles. In this way, the gauntlet is doubled and the cast-on rnd is fastened on the inside (56 sts).
Mitten: Knit around for 2 cm/¾ in for the wrist. Then inc

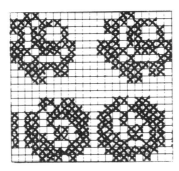

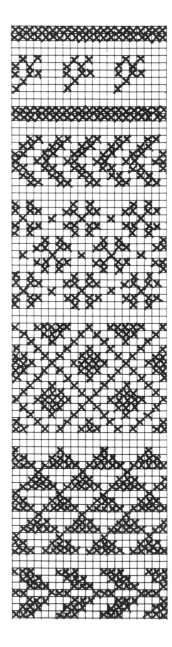

8 sts evenly spaced over 2 rnds (64 sts). If a pattern doesn't fit into the st count, inc or dec as necessary. Knit around in pattern. After 5 cm/2 in, put aside 15 sts for the thumb on a string or stitch holder. Cast on 15 sts above them and continue knitting around. When the mitten reaches the top of the little finger, dec 4 sts every rnd, 2 at each side. When 12 sts remain, draw the yarn through them and secure.

Thumb: Put the 15 sts of the thumb on a needle and pick up another 17 sts around the thumbhole. Divide the sts on three needles and knit around. Continue the pattern on the thumb. When the thumb reaches halfway up the thumbnail, dec 4 sts every rnd, 2 at each side. When 8 sts remain, draw the yarn through the sts and secure.

Gauntlet border: With a crochet hook, pick up 88 sts from the hole rnd on the gauntlet's turned edge. Divide them on dpn and work 3 rnds in k1, p1 ribbing. Bind off in ribbing.

Lovikka Mitten

Photo page 66
Size: Child's or woman's small
Yarn: unspun wool singles at about 1550 yd/lb (2375 m/kilo), 100 g/4 oz
Needles: Dpn 3.5/US 5

The mittens are knitted with two ends of the *kardband,* (sliver, roving, or unspun singles yarn) which are wound into a ball and knitted doubled (use the end from the inside and the end from the outside of the ball together).

Cast on 32 sts, evenly divided on four needles. Purl 2 rnds and then knit 9 rnds for the cuff. Turn the work so that the cuff's wrong side is facing out, then knit in stockinette for 10 cm/4 in. Set aside 7 sts for the thumb by knitting them with a piece of contrasting yarn. Continue for another 11 cm/4¼ in. Make sure there are the same number of sts on each needle. Begin decreasing with a ssk on the last 2 sts of each needle until 4 sts remain. Draw yarn through the sts and secure.

Thumb: Take out the contrasting yarn and pick up the 7 sts with one needle. Pick up the 7 sts above the thread + 1 st on each side. Divide onto three or four needles and do the decs as on the mitten top after about 8 cm/3¼ in.

Wash the mittens in water at 40° C (104° F) with a tablespoon of ammonia and some soap flakes. Handle carefully and don't rub. Rinse and let dry. Brush the surface with a steel brush or a carder. Begin working from the top of the inside and brush down toward the cuff. Turn the mitten and brush the outside in the same way. Don't brush the cuff sts so much that they can't be seen. Embroider the cuff with 2-ply wool yarn in two colors. Fasten a plait or cord made from *kardband* on the edge of the cuff. The cord can be finished with a tassel with the embroidery threads.

Beaded Wrist Warmers

Photo page 34
Size: Woman's
Yarn: 2-ply wool yarn at about 1600 yd/lb, 50 g/2 oz
Needles: Spn 2 mm/US 0; crochet hook 2 mm
Gauge: 27 sts and 30 rows = 10 cm/4 in

You will also need 2 bags of small beads and a needle for threading them.

The beaded wrist warmers are knitted in garter st as rectangles about 13 cm/5 in × 18 cm/7 in, then sewn into a ring and trimmed. The beads are drawn forward from the back side and sit on the strand between 2 sts. The beads are invisible on the inside of the finished wrist warmers.

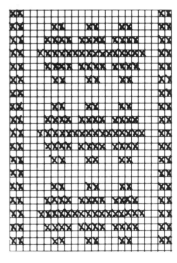

Begin by sketching a design on graph paper—the beads are knitted on every other row—and count out how many beads you need. (The pattern repeat corresponds to the wrist circumference.) The pattern shown here uses 76 × 8 = 608 beads for one wrist warmer. It's easiest to string the beads with a needle. If you want to use several colors of beads, string them in the correct order for the pattern!

Cast on 38 sts on spn 2 mm/US 0 and knit in garter st back and forth, slipping the 1st st on each row. Knit in the beads from the wrong side on every other row following the pattern until the piece measures about 18 cm/7 in. Bind off.

Turn the wrist warmer with the beads toward the inside and sew a side seam. Be sure that the pattern isn't obscured by the seam. Turn the wrist warmer and tightly crochet 1 row of sts on the hand edge and then crochet 1 row of picot sts.

Protest Cap

Photo page 50
Instructions written by Merete Lütken
Size: about 54 cm/21¼ in
Yarn: 3-ply wool yarn at about 1000 yd/lb, about 100 g/4 oz
Needles: Cn 40 cm, 2.5 mm and 3 mm/16 in, US 2 and 3, or the same size dpn
Gauge: 24 sts = 10 cm/4 in

Cast on 116 sts on cn 2.5 mm/US 2 and rib k1, p1 for about 3 cm/l¼ in. Change to cn 3 mm/US 3 and inc to 124 sts evenly spaced around. Knit in stockinette until the cap measures about 20 cm/8 in. Mark the sides of the cap, having the same number of sts on each side, and begin decs of 2 sts on each side of marker thus: k2 tog, k1, ssk. Repeat on the other side. Dec in this manner until 8 sts remain. Draw the yarn through the sts and secure. Make a cord with a tassel and sew it to the top of the cap.

Lace Wrist Warmers

Photo page 39
Instructions written by Elsa E. Guðjónsson. Taken from an Icelandic pattern from the first half of the twentieth century.
Size: Woman's
Yarn: 2-ply wool yarn at about 1600 yd/lb in 3–6 shades
Needles: Dpn 1.5 mm or 2 mm/US 00 or 0

The original wrist warmers, which were knitted in very fine handspun Icelandic wool, used six different natural colors: white, light gray, light brown, brown, dark brown, and natural black. They are knitted in the round with 96 sts and are 17 cm/6¾ in long. The ribbed cuff of 24 rnds is one-quarter of the length and the three six-color pattern repeats are worked over 72 rows for the remaining three-quarters of the length.

The instructions here require a heavier, commercially prepared yarn in fewer shades. Wrist warmer 1 uses three shades of brown or gray together with white or natural black and wrist warmer 2 uses only two shades and white or black.

Wrist warmer 1, four colors

Using the darkest color, cast on 72 sts. Divide the sts among three dpn (24 sts on each needle).
Rnd 1: *p1, k5*, repeat *–*.
Rnd 2: *p1, k2 tog, k3, yo, p1, yo, k3, ssk*, repeat *–*.

These rnds form the pattern. Knit 6 rnds with each of the four colors going from dark to light 2x: 48 rnds. Change to the darkest shade and work 18 rnds in k2, p2 ribbing. Bind off.

Wrist warmer 2, simple design, 3 colors

Cast on 60 sts. Knit 8 rnds with each color; otherwise, follow instructions above.

Skøleistur Slippers

Photo page 26
Instructions written by Nicolina Jensen. Design from Sørvåg.
Size: Adult
Yarn: 3-ply worsted weight wool yarn in two colors
Needles: Dpn 3.5 mm/US 5

Cast on 9 sts with the main color and knit the two-color pattern, following the diagram for the heel back and forth on dpn. When 20 rows have been knitted, pick up 18 sts along the sides of the heel. Now knit back and forth with three dpn in the combined patterns for another 28 rows, continuing the heel pattern on the bottom of the foot as shown in the diagram. Inc 1 st in each side. Knit another 6 rows and inc 1 st in each side.

Cast on 9 new sts for the top of the foot and knit the rest of the sock around on four dpn for 14 rows.

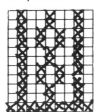

back of the heel 9 sts

Now begin the decs: *k1, ssk, knit to the end of the needle in pattern. On needle 2, knit the 2 last sts together. Needle 3: as needle 1; needle 4: as needle 2*. Work 1 rnd with decs *–*, 1 rnd without decs, and then dec on every rnd. When 12 sts remain, draw the yarn through the sts and secure. Weave in all loose ends.

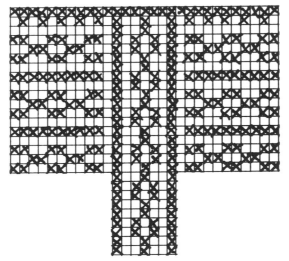

heel pattern joined to foot pattern

Nightcap

Photo page 18
Instructions by Kristina Lindkvist
Size: 54 (56) (58) cm/21¼ (22) (23) in
Yarn: Single-ply fingering wool at about 3200 yd/lb, 50 g/2 oz each red and white
Needles: Dpn 2 mm/US 0
Gauge: 32 sts = 10 cm/4 in

With white yarn, cast on 172 (180) (188) sts. Divide them on four needles and knit 1 rnd, purl 1 rnd. Now knit the check pattern on the turned-up edge in red and white.
Rnd 1: *k2 red, k2 white*, repeat *–*.
Rnds 2 and 3: *p2 red, k2 white*, repeat *–*.
Rnd 4: *k2 white, k2 red*, repeat *–*.
Rnds 5 and 6: *k2 white, p2 red*, repeat *–*.

Repeat rnds 1–3 another time and then knit 1 rnd white, 1 rnd red, 1 rnd white.

Purl 1 rnd white, knit 1 rnd white for the turning rows. Continue in stockinette and white yarn for 2 cm/¾ in. Turn the cap inside out at the purl turning row and, using white, continue in stockinette for 2.5 cm/1 in. The rest of the cap is knitted in stockinette *3 red rnds, 3 white rnds, 3 red rnds, 3 white rnds, 3 red rnds*, then white for 2 cm/¾ in. Repeat *–* once more and then knit 2.5 cm/1 in in white.

Top shaping: *K3, k2 tog*, repeat *–*. Knit the next rnd without decreasing. Next: *k2, k2 tog*, repeat *–*. Next rnd: no decs. Next: *k1, k2 tog*, repeat *–*. No decs on the next rnd. Next: *k2 tog around and then work one rnd without decs*, repeat *–* until about 8 sts remain. Draw the yarn through the sts. Make a tassel and sew it on.

Jomala Cap

Photo page 70
Instructions written by Anne-Marie Rinne-Vest

Circumference: 52 cm/20½ in

Yarn: 2-ply fine fingering weight wool yarn in madder red, green, blue, and black

Needles: Cn 40 cm, 2 mm/16 in, US 0

Gauge: 35 sts = 10 cm/4 in

Cast on 156 sts and knit 12 rnds in stockinette with the main color (madder red). Knit pattern I with green stripes and figures on a madder red background. Then knit 37 rnds in main color. Knit 9 rnds blue and 4 rnds main color.

Knit pattern II with madder red figures on a black background. Knit 4 rnds main color and 9 rnds blue.

Knit pattern III with green on a madder red background and then 4 rnds main color.

Knit pattern IV with green figures on a red background and then 4 rnds in main color.

Knit pattern III with green on a red background, then 12 rnds main color.

Knit pattern II with madder red figures on a black background. The top shaping begins on the last rnd of this repeat of pattern II. Knit 30 rnds in main color, shaping the top.

Top shaping: At four evenly spaced places, k2 tog, k1, k2 tog. Decs are made on every 4th rnd 4x and then on every other rnd 15x. Draw thread through sts and secure.

Entrelac Knitting

What is special about *entrelac* (basketweave) knitting is that every square of the pattern is completely knitted before the next one is begun. The technique is especially suitable for stockings and other garments which need quite a bit of elasticity.

It is easiest to work on a cn.

Using dark yarn, cast on 66 sts on a cn: 11 squares with 6 sts each. You need an uneven number of squares so that two squares of the same color don't come together when you're knitting in the round. Knit one rnd after casting-on rnd.

The 1st rnd is formed with half squares: Knit 2 sts, turn (from now on, slip the 1st st on both right and wrong sides) and purl back. Turn, k3 sts, turn again and purl them back. Turn, knit 4 sts, turn and purl back. Turn and knit 5 sts, turn and purl back. Turn and knit 6 sts, turn and purl back. When all 6 sts of the square are knitted, work back and forth once more before beginning the next square.

Knit 2 sts, turn and purl back, knit 3 sts, turn, and so forth until the whole 1st rnd of half squares is finished.

The next rnd forms whole squares. The sts are picked up along the right-hand edge of the half squares. Although these are knitted back and forth an extra time, they lose an edge st. So that there will be 6 sts, pick up a 6th st from the casting-on rnd. Pick up the edge sts in the back loop with the left needle (or pick them up with the right and transfer them to the left). The wrong side should be facing you.

Begin with the light color and purl the sts. After the 1st row, slip the 1st st. Turn and knit back. Turn and purl until 1 st remains, purl it together with 1 st from the 2nd square row in dark yarn. Turn and knit back, turn and purl until 1 st remains, purl it together with a dark st from the next square. Continue in this manner until

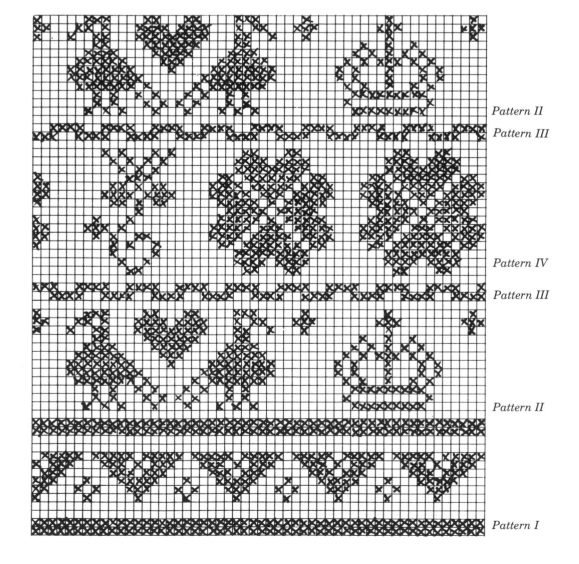

Pattern II
Pattern III

Pattern IV

Pattern III

Pattern II

Pattern I

all sts of the dark square are taken up. Pick up new edge sts from the next square in the previous rnd and work in the same way. When all the squares of this rnd are knitted, change colors again and knit the next rnd. Finish with a rnd of half squares.

Star-Pattern Man's Stocking

Photo page 53
Instructions from Rauma
Size: Man's large
Yarn: 3-ply wool yarn at about 1000 yd/lb, 200 g/7 oz each dark and light
Needles: Dpn 2.5 mm/US 2
Gauge: 34 sts and 38 rows = 10 cm/4 in

Cast on 88 sts with the dark yarn and work k2, p2 ribbing for 10 rnds. Inc evenly over the next rnd to 92 sts and knit 8 rnds in stockinette. Then begin the pattern following the diagram. After 8 pattern rnds, inc 2 sts every other rnd 6 times. The incs are made at the back between the 2 seed-pattern lines.

Knit another 26 rnds and then begin decreasing 2 sts every 3rd rnd until all the sts between the seed-pattern lines plus 1 of the seed lines are finished. Then dec 2 sts at the narrow side patterns every 5th rnd until there is only 1 st left between the seed pattern lines.

Now continue without decreasing. After 4½ large patterns at the front, divide the work for the heel. Put the 30 sts of the center back on one needle. Put the instep sts aside on a string. Work back and forth in the background pattern (2 black, 2 white for 2 rows, then white over black, and vice versa). Knit 24 rows in this way (12 edge sts). Now begin decreasing for the heel on the wrong side. Mark center. Purl to center. Purl next 2 sts tog, p1, turn. Sl 1st st, work to center, ssk, k1, turn. Continue dec this way using 1 st on each side of the "hole" until all st are used. Begin the gusset.

Star-Patterned Man's Stocking　　　　　　　　　　　*Center Back*

Pick up 12 sts on one side of the heel along with half of the heel sts with one needle and pick up the rest of the heel sts and the 12 edge sts on the other side with a second needle. The instep sts are divided onto two needles. Knit 1 rnd, twisting the picked-up edge sts. The instep sts are knitted in pattern following the diagram while the rest of the sts are knitted in the checkered background pattern.

Make decs every other rnd by k2 tog at the end of the first heel needle and begin with ssk on the fourth needle.

When 74 sts are left, knit around without decreasing. After 6½ large patterns have been knitted, dec 6 sts evenly over the instep sts and then knit the whole foot in the checkered background pattern. Continue until the stocking reaches the little toe. Knit every 6th and 7th sts together on the next rnd. Knit 6 rnds. Then knit together every 5th and 6th sts, then every 4th and 5th sts and so forth with 5, 4, 3, rnds between dec rnds, until 10 sts remain. Draw yarn through the sts and secure.

APPENDIX

Conversion Chart For Yarn Weights and Measurements

WEIGHT (Rounded to nearest ¼ oz)		LENGTH (to nearest ¼ in)			
g	oz	cm	in	cm	in
25	1	1	½	55	21¾
50	2	2	¾	60	23½
100	3¾	3	1¼	65	25½
150	5½	4	1½	70	27½
200	7¼	5	2	75	29½
250	9	6	2½	80	31½
300	10¾	7	2¾	85	33½
350	12½	8	3	90	35½
400	14¼	9	3½	95	37½
450	16	10	4	100	39½
500	17¾	11	4¼	110	43½
550	19½	12	4¾	120	47
600	21¼	13	5	130	51¼
650	23	14	5½	140	55
700	24¾	15	6	150	59
750	26½	16	6¼	160	63
800	28¼	17	6¾	170	67
850	30	18	7	180	70¾
900	31¾	19	7½	190	74¾
950	33	20	8	200	78¼
1000	35½	25	9¾	210	82¾
1200	42¼	30	11¾	220	86½
1400	49¼	35	13¾	230	90½
1600	56½	40	15¾	240	94½
1800	63½	45	17¾	250	98½
2000	70½	50	19¾	300	118

Conversion Chart For Needle Sizes

Needle sizes given in the patterns are recommended as starting points for you to make your gauge (tension) samples before you begin to knit the garment. If you can't obtain the given gauge (tension), try a different needle size. It really is well worth going to the trouble of matching gauge (tension); care taken at this stage will prevent needless disappointment later from strangely sized garments.

METRIC	US	OLD UK
2 mm	0	14
2.25 mm	1	13
2.5 mm		
2.75 mm	2	12
3 mm		11
3.25 mm	3	10
3.5 mm	4	
3.75 mm	5	9
4 mm	6	8
4.5 mm	7	7
5 mm	8	6
5.5 mm	9	5
6 mm	10	4
6.5 mm	10½	3
7 mm		2
7.5 mm		1
8 mm	11	0
9 mm	13	00
10 mm	15	000

Comparative Terms

US	UK
Bind off	Cast off
Every other row	Alternate rows
Gauge	Tension
Stockinette stitch	Stocking stitch

(Other terms are the same in both countries.)

Yarn Equivalents

The following table lists the equivalent US and UK yarns in terms of thickness. When substituting yarns, it is essential that you check gauge (tension) before you buy enough for the whole garment.

US	UK
Sport	4 ply
Knitting worsted	Double knitting (DK)
Fisherman	Aran weight
Bulky	Chunky

Substitute Yarns For UK Knitters

Faroese Sweater: *Rowan Designer Collection Double Knitting Wool in shade 62 (black) and shade 60 (grey)*

Greenland Sweater: *Rowan Designer Collection Double Knitting Wool in shade 62 (black) and shade 2 (cream)*

Setesdal Sweater: *Rowan Designer Collection Double Knitting Wool in shade 62 (black) and shade 110 (white)*

Seed-Patterned Pörtom Sweater: *Rowan Designer Collection Double Knitting Wool in shade 62 (black), shade 110 (white), and shade 98 (brown)*

Ullared Sweater: *Jamieson & Smith 2-ply Lace Weight wool in shade L45 (rust) and shade L77 (black)*

Spjäll (Gusset) Sweater: *Jamieson & Smith 2-ply Lace Weight wool in shade L93 (red) and shade L135 (blue)*

Cotton Pörtom Sweater: *Twilleys of Stamford Lyscordet No 5 100% mercerized cotton in shade 21 (unbleached white), shade 30 (red), and shade 61 (blue)*

Fisherman Sweater in Linen or Hair-Blend Yarn: *Rowan Aran in Natural wool; unspun natural flax from Frank Herring & Sons*

Child's Sweater with Patterns from Vörä: *Twilleys of Stamford Lyscordet No 5 100% mercerized cotton in shade 21 (unbleached white) and shade 61 (blue)*

Lopi Sweater: *Lopi 100% wool in shade 0059 (black), shade 0058 (mid-grey), and shade 0056 (light grey)*

Boy's Cardigan—Setesdal Pattern: *Rowan Designer Collection Double Knitting Wool in shade 97 (blue) and shade 110 (white)*

Sweater with Selbu Patterns: *Rowan Designer Collection Double Knitting Wool in shade 604 (brown) and shade 110 (white)*

Korsnäs Sweater: *Falcon 3-ply Superwash pure new wool in shade 2742 (Pennant red), shade 2705 (Glen green), shade 2747 (Banana yellow), shade 2701 (Begonia red), and shade 2725 (White)*

Fana Cardigan: *Rowan Designer Collection Double Knitting Wool in shade 62 (black) and shade 110 (white)*

Ljusdal Cardigan: *Jamieson & Smith 2-ply Jumper Weight wool in shade 125 (red), shade 1 (white), and shade 83 (green)*

Jacket with Knitted Sleeves: *Jamieson & Smith 2-ply Lace Weight wool in shade L5 (black) and shade L42 (brown)*

Night Sweater: *Falcon Guernsey wool in shade A803 (Navy)*

Triangular Shawl: *Jamieson & Smith 3-ply wool in shade H44 (Indigo)*

Selbu Mitten: *Rowan Designer Collection Double Knitting Wool in shade 110 (white) and shade 604 (brown)*

Faroese Lace Pattern Shawl: *Rowan Designer Collection Double Knitting Wool in shade 129 (brown)*

Selbu Glove: *Rowan Designer Collection Double Knitting wool in shade 110 (white) and shade 604 (brown)*

Mitten with a Pattern from Tjöck: *Jamieson & Smith 2-ply Jumper Weight wool in shade 77 (black), shade 18 (blue), shade FC11 (green), shade 93 (scarlet), and shade 1 (white)*

Checkerboard Mitten from Jutland: *Jamieson & Smith 2-ply Jumper Weight wool in shade 77 (black) and shade 1 (white)*

Man's Mitten from Varanger: *Jamieson & Smith 2-ply Jumper Weight wool in shade 17 (blue), shade 1 (white), and shade 93 (scarlet)*

Gauntlet Mitten with Gotland Patterns: *Jamieson & Smith 2-ply Jumper Weight wool in shade 1 (white) and shade 21 (blue)*

Lovikka Mitten: *Lopi 100% wool in shade 0061 (cream)*

Beaded Wrist Warmers: *Jamieson & Smith 2-ply Lace Weight wool in shade 125 (red)*

Protest Cap: *Jamieson & Smith 3-ply wool in shade H92 (red)*

Lace Wrist Warmers: *Jamieson & Smith 2-ply Jumper Weight wool in shade 203 (light grey), shade 27 (dark grey), shade 4 (brown), shade 5 (black), and shade 1 (white)*

Skøleistur Slippers: *Rowan Designer Collection Double Knitting Wool in shade 110 (white) and shade 604 (brown)*

Night Cap: *Jamieson & Smith 2-ply Lace Weight wool in shade L93 (scarlet) and shade L1a (cream)*

Jomala Cap: *Jamieson & Smith 2-ply Lace Weight wool in shade L125 (madder red), shade L77 (black), shade L18 (blue), and shade L8 (green)*

Star Pattern Man's Stocking: *Rowan Designer Collection Double Knitting Wool in shade 62 (black) and shade 110 (white)*

UK Suppliers

Colourway
112a Westbourne Grove
(entrance on Chepstow Road)
London W2 5RU
Alafoss Lopi 100% Wool

Falcon Yarns
Falcon-by-post
Westfield Road
Horbury
Wakefield
West Yorkshire WF4 6HD
Falcon 3-Ply Superwash Wool, Falcon Guernsey Wool

Frank Herring & Sons
27 High West Road
Dorchester
Dorset DT1 1UP
Unspun flax, wool sliver

Jamieson & Smith (Shetland Wool Brokers) Ltd
90 North Road
Lerwick
Shetland Isles ZE1 0PQ
Jamieson & Smith 2-Ply Lace Weight Wool, Jamieson & Smith 2-Ply Jumper Weight Wool, Jamieson & Smith 3-Ply Wool

Rowan Yarns
Green Lane Mill
Washpit
Holmfirth
West Yorkshire HD7 1RW
Rowan Designer Collection Double Knitting Wool, Rowan Aran in Natural Wool

Twilleys of Stamford
Roman Mills
Stamford
Lincolnshire PE9 1BG
Twilleys of Stamford Lyscordet No 5 100% Mercerized Cotton

INDEX